Mobile Marketing:

101 Inexpensive and Profitable

Ideas for Small Business

by

Mitchell Cogert

Mobile Marketing:
101 Inexpensive and Profitable
Ideas for Small Business

By Mitchell Cogert

©2011 All rights reserved
ISBN: 1460920295

For more information go to:
www.FirstMobileWebsite.com

TABLE OF CONTENTS

Introduction

Mobile marketing is a hot topic for companies of all sizes that want to reach out to customers in new, innovative ways. Consider the fact that there are over 275 million mobile phone subscribers in the U.S., and that over 100 million of them are using the mobile web from their devices. That's a lot of people, and a huge opportunity for your small business.

At its simplest, mobile marketing is the communication of consumers via mobile device, be it a phone, PDA or tablet. Through mobile marketing, companies transmit simple marketing messages that introduce consumers to new products and offers, entice them to participate in campaigns, or allow them to visit a mobile website.

What Makes Mobile Different

Mobile consumers aren't like TV viewers or web surfers, both of which have become desensitized to the advertisements that bombard them all day long. Advertising messages come at them from all sides, and even the most valuable, innovative messages are often overlooked. Consumers have gotten to the point where they ignore most of the attacks, choosing instead to fast forward through TV commercials and/or flip past full-page magazine ads.

But cell phones are hard to ignore, and have become the communication tool for many. These devices not only take and receive calls, but they also put people in touch with friends via text messaging, and allow them to manage email accounts and handle myriad other tasks on the fly. These mobile users are open to new ideas, even when these suggestions come hurtling at them over their cellular carrier's network.

Why am I telling you all of this? Because mobile spells opportunity, and it comes in an affordable, simple package that small business owners can't ignore any longer. Whether your company wants to attract new consumers, grow its opt-in customer database, sell more products or services, or build brand awareness, mobile marketing is the perfect addition to an existing marketing strategy. In fact, it goes hand-in-hand with other marketing methods without cannibalizing them, and will help elevate your small business to new levels.

I know this because I've seen firsthand the positive effects that mobile marketing campaigns can have on the companies that use them, and the consumers that participate in them. A small pizza shop that increases its sales by 10% by sending out coupons to a list of opt-in, "VIP" customers, for example, not only sells more food, but it also builds one of the most valuable tools that any business can have: a database of loyal, valued customers that <u>want</u> to receive information and special offers. This two-way street also works the other way around when those same clients participate in surveys and offer valuable feedback that you can use to hone your business strategy.

Less expensive than many other marketing mediums, and fairly simple to set up and use, mobile marketing is still new terrain for most small businesses. But with billions of SMS text messages being transmitted every month worldwide – and with even more predicted for the future – it won't be long before everyone from the sole proprietor who is hawking sports memorabilia to the 500-employee equipment manufacturer jumps into the mobile marketing fray.

After all, who can resist using a marketing tool that's affordable, easy to use, untapped and proven? No one.

Mobile Marketing=Sales

Why should you be thinking about mobile marketing right now? Chances are, you cut back on advertising and marketing during the economic downturn (don't feel bad because you're in good company). The move helped you save a few bucks, but sales and lead generation suffered as a result. Your customer pipeline is all but empty, and you're scrambling to get it beefed back up to pre-recession levels. To get there, you want to try some new, affordable, effective marketing strategies. You know mobile is hot, but you're not sure how to implement it in a way that benefits your company.

As you'll learn throughout this book, you're not alone. Many companies are already experimenting with mobile and seeing positive results from their efforts. You'll read about restaurants that are using mobile coupons, event planners that rely on text messaging campaigns to get new users to opt into their member databases, retailers that are using mobile to lure in new customers, online portals that have invested in mobile campaigns to increase traffic to their sites, and hardware stores that are using text message campaigns to attract new customers to their bricks-and-mortar locations. The list goes on...

These companies are achieving many of the same goals and objectives you've set for your own small business, and they're doing it with one or more of the following methods, each of which is covered in depth in this book:

- Mobile website
- SMS or text messaging
- Mobile advertising
- Location-based mobile social media
- Proximity marketing
- Mobile apps
- QR codes

To help you choose among these seven different areas, and decide which will best fit your own marketing approach, we've broken this book down into seven parts, each of which addresses a specific mobile marketing technique. We'll introduce you to the idea, and then show you exactly how to use it successfully in your own business. By reading how other companies are using mobile marketing, you'll be able to put the same strategies to work in your company immediately.

When you've finished reading this book, you'll know what the top mobile marketing tools are, how much they cost to implement and use, and how businesses like yours can implement these tools to spur company growth, create brand awareness, build a client database and achieve various other goals.

Throughout this book, we'll give you the information you need to get a mobile marketing campaign rolling at your own company, and help you make the best possible decisions regarding your ongoing efforts in this area. A list of trusted providers included at the end of the book, for example, will help you launch your search for third parties to get your campaign "mobilized."

If you're ready to get started, flip to the next section of this book and we'll show you how a mobile website is a necessity for your business; that is, if your customers carry a phone with them.

A Mobile Website is at the Heart of Going Mobile

There are over 4.2 billion mobile phones in the world. There are 80 million smartphone users in the US. A consumer on a mobile phone is three times more likely to buy a product than on a computer desktop. And, yet, most businesses ignore the sales opportunity by letting customers view their current website on a mobile phone. This is a mistake.

Let me explain why you need a mobile website that complements your current website.

Your current website has been built to be accessed by a desktop computer via the Internet. Your website has the luxury of being as in-depth and comprehensive as possible. You can use long copy, audio and video to inform, entertainment and convince visitors to buy your products and services. This Internet connection to your desktop computer can handle as much data as you want. And, the consumer can sit back and browse your site at his leisure.

Things are very different in the mobile web environment.

First, the customer on the mobile web is on the move. He does not have the time to read long copy or to explore your site in-depth. He is arriving on your website from the most personal device he owns--his phone. He may be interrupted by a personal or business call. He may be en route to a destination. He may be pressed for time.

Most customers who access your site from a mobile device will know what they want, and they will need that information now. Other customers may have more time to browse your site, but the environment is different as they are using a mobile device.

Second, a mobile device has a smaller screen size. If you put your current website on your phone you will find that it is okay, and maybe even good. But, good enough is not enough for your business.

You see, many websites are actually cutoff when viewed on a mobile phone. The formatting of information on a mobile site requires proper design.

Here are some general guidelines:

- Your mobile site needs to be easy to navigate; no desired information can be more than three clicks away.

- Your information must be "snackable;" this is short, bite-sized chunks.

- Your content must connect with a customer on the move searching for an answer now. I call it "actionable" content such as a click to call button, your address, maps, and driving directions.

One study states that 86% of consumers are unhappy with the performance of websites when they access them on their mobile phone. That research screams opportunity for your business to standout from your competition.

Third, there are over 500 different types of mobile devices. Your website has been optimized to work on a few platforms like a PC or Mac. Mobile devices are all over the place as there are cell phones based on the Android, iPhone, Blackberry, and more. While optimization of a mobile website is more difficult, it can be done.

If you want to build loyalty, traffic and sales to an audience of customers who are on the move, a mobile website is the way to go. It is the heart of any mobile strategy.

Here is one way to distinguish a desktop based website and a mobile website. A desktop-based website should be "phat and happy." A mobile website should be "fast and easy."

Here are some of the key components of a "fast and easy" mobile website:

- Maps
- Driving directions
- Business hours
- Click to call button
- Products/Special offers
- Tell a friend form
- Opt-in forms
- Mcommerce

Hot Off the Press (January 2011): Wow! Consumers plan on using their mobile devices as much or more than their desktop computer for shopping information (conducted by Yahoo! and The Nielsen Company).

In the next 12 months, the consumers use of mobile devices and desktop computers for accessing shopping information:

Category	Mobile vs Desktop PC
Entertainment items and content:	73% vs 60%
Restaurants/dining:	73% vs 52%
Digital content for a mobile phone:	73% vs 28%
Financial services:	66% vs 58%
Consumer electronics and technology:	61% vs 57%
Personal or vacation travel:	58% vs 52%
Clothing apparel & fashion accessories:	57% vs 56%
Healthcare or medical related:	48% vs 57%
Packaged food and beverage:	47% vs 46%
Beauty and personal care:	46% vs 43%
Home improvement:	44% vs 57%
Automobiles or auto parts or access:	41% vs 43%

This is truly remarkable data. A mobile website is more of an opportunity in the next 12 months than ever before.

In the following section, I have highlighted mobile websites that had to turn a "phat and happy" website into a "fast and easy" one. While most of these mobile sites are from big companies, it may provide you with ideas on how you can build your own mobile website. Frankly, if they can cut down thousands of pages for a mobile site, you should be able to do the same for yours.

Note: A mobile website is not to be confused with a mobile applications. A mobile application must be downloaded into your device, while a mobile website does not. We will cover mobile applications in more depth later on.

Restaurants

1. What's for Dinner?

When you are out on the town, you may be looking for a place to eat. Among consumers who use their mobile device to get restaurant information, there is a need for the following:

- Restaurant location: 75%
- Finding the location of the restaurant: 73%

- Deciding where to eat: 54%
- Looking up a menu: 56%
- Clicking to call (39%).

The Zagat mobile website delivers this information and more. Their site is clean and easy to use. You pick a city, a zip code, address, intersection, city or intended city to find a place to eat. You can even search by the restaurant name or a keyword. The results appear from your search and you are on your way to your next meal. This is all for free. If you want reviews and ratings, they provide a premium paid service.

What's important to take away is that the Zagat mobile website delivers what a customer on the move wants. They even can generate revenue by offering a premium service.

2. Pizza to Go, On the Go.

The Pepe's Pizza mobile site is another one that connects with the customer on the move. This site is all about making the customer experience friendly. It delivers in more ways than just on the promise of delicious pizza, delivered right to your door.

The site is a menu that makes selection of items and ordering easy. It adds a click to call button on the home page, and "above the fold." What this means is that the customer does not have to scroll around to search for a way to order. It is big, upfront, and simple to use.

If the customer wants to visit one of their locations, the site has a map with driving directions. This is familiar to anyone who uses driving directions. You click on driving directions and the screen asks you to enter your current position. Instantly, you will see a map, the route, and the time it takes to get from Point A to Point B.

3. A Happy Meal.

Here is a mobile site that is all about location, location, and location. The McDonald's mobile site in the UK is a McDonald's restaurant locator. When you visit the company's mobile site, it detects your location and posts the address of the nearest McDonald's.

Is there a menu on their site? No. I guess McDonalds knows you know what they have to eat for breakfast, lunch and dinner.

Sports

4. ESPN Scores.

The ESPN site is another winner. It almost breaks the rules about "snackable" content, since fans by definition are fanatics about their sports teams.

The ESPN website is packed with more information than you will ever be able read or watch. Well, at least, that I will be ever to read or watch.

While ESPN understands that the mobile web is different, it also knows that its customers have an intense desire for the latest sports news in general and on their team, an up-to-date scoreboard, video highlights, statistics and more. The fantasy sports craze has added for a fans need to know.

ESPN built their mobile website to get the information you want whether you have only seconds to visit their site or minutes. It is quite a feat.

It combines the ease of navigation with the speed to access information. It gives the sports fan the option for a quick hit up the middle with the option to go deep. If you are a fan, I am sure you have checked out the site.

Visiting the ESPN mobile site the first time, I was concerned that I would be hit with a slow download since their desktop PC website is filled with so many graphics and videos. That is not that case here at all. The home page downloads fast on a mobile device. It lists upfront the most recent sports news along with up-to-date scores. And, if you want more, it feeds it to you, the way you want it.

Entertainment

5. Movie Magic

One of the great benefits of being on the phone is the built-in GPS. If you allow a site to access your current location, you can get added benefits that you never had before. The McDonald's restaurant locator mobile site is an example.

Another example of this benefit to having GPS on your phone is the Moviefone mobile site. When you visit the Moviefone site, when you allow it to access your current location, it presents the movies that are playing nearby. It is very cool. It is very convenient. It is very easy.

When you build your mobile website make it a mobile friendly one. Think about the needs of your mobile customer first, and then how your site can connect to those needs. It is marketing 101, taken to mobile website marketing 101.

Media

6. Mobile Handset Detection

Here is a feature to add to your current website that will do your business good.

When a consumer is on his mobile phone, he may make the error of typing in your desktop computer website URL, rather than your mobile site address. For example, he may be on his iPhone and he enters www.yourcompany.com.

When this happens, your website should automatically connect that consumer to your mobile friendly site.

An example of this feature is with CNN. When a consumer is on his phone, he may put in www.cnn.com instead of the CNN mobile website address. Rather than allowing a visitor to have a sub-optimal experience with their news service, the website auto-detects that the visitor is on his mobile phone and takes him to the CNN mobile site.

Not every business knows they can have this feature on their websites. It really is simple to do and it will add to a positive experience for your customers.

Did you know that Google detects which device you are using to conduct searches? If you are on a mobile device, the search results give preference to mobile websites. The area of mobile search will be covered later in the book. It is interesting since it gives the small, local business an opportunity to be found on Page 1 for result ahead of the big name brands.

Services

7. Put the Weather in Your Pocket.

For some reason, The Weather Channel can mesmerize me on television. Well, to my dismay, I discovered The Weather Channel website on my iPad.

The Weather Channel is another example of a mobile site that delivers what you need, fast. I guess that is a good thing if a tornado is headed your way.

Their mobile site provides all your local weather information, and of course, there is so much more to explore. It answers questions you may have about how the weather may affect your travel plans or outdoor activities.

One feature on this site that may lead you to something similar on your site is their mobile alert system. The Weather Channel site allows you to sign up for weather alerts. Your mobile site may ask consumers to sign up for special coupon offers, deals or announcements. It is an excellent way to build a mobile database to use for marketing.

8. Just the Recipes, Please.

One of the more interesting ways to build a mobile site has been developed by allrecipes.com. Their website is filled with information and photos on the home page that will make you hungry.

On their mobile website, their home page is barren. It is a search bar that allows you to look up a recipe or your favorite ingredients. The results from your search appear so you are only one click away to that appetizing, new recipe. It doesn't get much simpler than this. The site is mobile.allrecipes.com.

9. When You Gotta Go…

Yes, mobility can mean a lot of different things. However, it means the same thing when you must locate a restroom.

The mobile site is MizPee and it helps you find a place to go when you are on the go. MizPee gives you the closest, cleanest toilet when you need one. It also provides entertaining reading material when you get there. The site is still in Beta, but I hope it catches on. Anything that can help clean up the mess in the streets of San Francisco is a good thing.

Retail

10. Shop and Save

When Fatwallet.com decided to address the mobile user, their executives must have had some interesting meetings. After all, Fatwallet's website is "phat" and fully-loaded with coupons, more coupons, and more coupons.

The Fatwallet mobile website has been streamlined, to say the least. Fatwallet selected only one section of its impressive website for their mobile site. The mobile site is the forum section of their PC-based site. The forum has coupons, coupons and more coupons, but they are only from their members. Of course, their membership is in the millions, so it's not like you won't find a good deal.

One mobile tactic that Fatwallet may want to consider is QR codes. We will get more into that later in the book.

SMS or Text Messaging

When you think of SMS (which stands for short message service) or text messaging, your first thought probably goes to the short notes you send back and forth between friends via your cell phone. Going to be late for dinner? Better let your spouse know via a short text. Running late for work and stuck in traffic? Your co-workers can get a quick heads up via SMS. The approach works pretty well in most cases, and has all but replaced the handset as a way to communicate in short bursts.

What you may not realize is that the medium is also an effective and low-cost way to boost traffic to your website and increase sales.

In fact, text messaging is mobile marketing's backbone. Using 160-character, alphanumeric messages, companies can announce special deals, build customer loyalty and fill in the "gaps" when business slows. These campaigns are fairly simple to launch and administer, and return fast results because over 90% of text messages are read within five minutes of receipt (unlike email, which can languish in someone's inbox for days, or worse yet, "scroll up" and never be opened).

As the most commonly used phone method in the U.S., SMS even works on phones that lack Internet access (since the messages go across the mobile network, and not the Internet, like email does). Your recipient doesn't need an iPhone or Blackberry to be able to receive and respond to your message – any old cell phone will do.

Here's how SMS marketing works:

> Using 6-digit Common Short Codes (CSC) or abbreviated phone numbers, you prompt users to "opt in" to a campaign, special offer or membership. At that point, that consumer becomes a willing recipient of future SMS campaigns (The Mobile Marketing Association prohibits companies from sending mobile messages to consumers unless they opt-in).

If the simplicity of SMS marketing isn't enough to sell you on the idea, here's another benefit: Text messaging is affordable. The small business that sends out 500 text messages per month, for example, will pay about $5.00 per month for the marketing campaign. That's less than one cent per message – a paltry sum when compared to other types of direct-to-consumer advertising (a similar direct mail campaign, for example, can cost $500 or more).

Text messaging is also universal, and applicable in many different marketing situations. Use it to attract customers to your products and services at the point where they're ready to buy; hit hard-to-reach prospects that are immune to other advertising methods; collect email addresses for your customer database; or send timely alerts that you <u>know</u> will be opened and read within just a few minutes (unlike direct mail, which can sit unopened on the recipient's kitchen counter for weeks!).

Whatever your goal, some aspect of SMS marketing will address it. Here are a few more benefits that you can expect from an SMS campaign:

✓ Real-time delivery.

>Recipients get your message just a few seconds after you hit send, and most open them within five minutes or less.

✓ Significant reach with little or no additional investment.

>The number of mobile phone users is on the rise, but the amount of money it takes to create and execute a campaign remains constant.

✓ Cost-effective.

>For small companies looking to hit their current and prospective clients when they are on the move, there simply isn't any better option than mobile.

✓ Good response.

>People aren't "immune" to text messaging yet, so response rates for this type of advertising remain high.

✓ Accountable.

>You can easily determine how effective your SMS campaigns are, and then tweak them accordingly.

You can take your SMS campaign a step further by using MMS (Multimedia Messaging Services) to add images, audio, video or rich text to your campaign. Tell a story, give recipients a glimpse into something special or share a valuable video tip with your prospects and your chances of getting a positive response could increase exponentially.

Text Messaging in Action

The best way to learn about a new marketing technique is by example. That's why this book is filled with case studies that show how other companies are already successfully using one or more mobile marketing methods.

When you can actually <u>see</u> how others are successfully utilizing a new method, it becomes that much easier to integrate into your own program. You can learn from their successes and mistakes, and have a much better chance of avoiding the latter.

We'll start with a few good examples of text messaging in action. Through these case studies, you'll see how other businesses are using it for simple information messaging, rewards programming, coupons and even direct response advertising. By the way, we group examples by industry so that you can quickly locate those that best relate to your own needs, although we encourage you to read through all of them as each has its own nuances and nuggets of advice to share.

Food and Beverage

11. Will That Be Cheese or Pepperoni?

Many restaurant chains have discovered the value of mobile marketing, with text messaging being one of the most popular methods they are using. Papa John's is one the most prolific users of text messaging campaigns in the restaurant industry, where hitting the consumer with the right offer and at the right time can mean the difference between selling a pizza, or watching the consumer buy one from your competitor a few miles away.

At the heart of the Papa John's mobile strategy is an ordering system that it implemented a few years ago. The system allows users to order pizza via text message, and it reportedly brought in an additional $1 million in revenue within six months of implementation. Today, about 20% of the pizza chain's sales come from mobile, SMS and smartphones.

Here's the chain's process:

1. Customers register online at www.papajohns.com and save their favorite orders, delivery and payment preferences with the Papa John's "Favorites Wizard."

2. Once registered online, the Papa John's consumer can simply text FAV1, FAV2, and so forth, to 4PAPA (47272).

3. Papa John's then sends a text message detailing the order and requesting confirmation from the consumer.

4. The consumer presses Y1 to confirm the order for FAV1 or N1 to change the order. Once confirmed, the closest Papa John's restaurant processes the order.

By allowing its customers to order via text message from their cell phones, Papa John's is not only saving itself money and time (spent on the phone with customers taking orders, for example), but it's also building a mobile database of loyal customers who are open to receiving coupons, special offers and exclusive savings now and in the future via text messaging.

12. Waffles, Anyone?

With a quirky building style and reliable menu, Waffle House holds an iconic place in the heart of the typical American, few of which have missed the opportunity to try the restaurant's breakfast food at least once in their lifetime.

To build on its existing reputation, Waffle House launched its first 2-way SMS text marketing campaign in 2010, and posted a 47% increase in opt-in subscribers during the first 30 days of the effort.

"We get a lot of travelers who come eat with us- so the 2-way SMS text locator gives customers who are on the road the ability to still find us wherever they are," said a Waffle House spokesperson. "With the way technology is developing it was a good opportunity to give our customers another way to find our restaurants."

To use the program consumers must text the word WH and their zip code or city, state to LOCATE (562283) to find their closest restaurant.

With 1,600 restaurants spanning 25 states, Waffle House does much of its advertising via local, grassroots efforts. "Waffle House is not known as a technology-driven company, so for us this text program is a very big step," said the spokesperson.

In fact with only two opt-in points (out of a planned seven) currently in-use, plus Waffle House's corporate website and marketing collateral at the restaurants, the text marketing program has already exceeded its expectations.

13. If It's Free, It's for Me.

Using text messaging to offer special promotions to diners is an especially effective way to get people in the door, as one retail franchise owner recently learned. To entice customers, the dessert shop owner created numerous "call to action" notices that were displayed on tabletops, banners, bulletin boards and windows.

On the signs, the shop owner offered customers "Free Yogurt" to all whom texted a 6-digit short code to a specific short code number. Eager to get their reward, customers pulled out their mobile phones and started texting.

The restaurant's owner trained his staff on how to get customers to opt into the program, which was free, of course. Once the customer took that step and submitted the short code, a welcome text message was sent out, which included the store's phone number (to identify the specific franchise location that developed the campaign) and information about the free yogurt offer.

According to the franchise owner, the campaign resulted in 500+ opt-ins. And, he is now using that list to send out even more offers, and to generate viral participation among his customers' friends, family and co-workers. Not too shabby of a return for a campaign that was relatively simple to execute, and that helped the store beef up its customer database 500-fold.

14. A "Fresh" Approach.

Subway is another franchise that is not afraid to test out new marketing methods. When one of its multi-location franchisees wanted to expand its customer base and generate more business, the franchise came up with its "My Subway Mobile" program.

The mobile campaign was advertised via brochures, and on the radio and television in the restaurant's local market area. Special product offers and coupons that could only be accessed via text message or email drew customers in, urging them to pick up their cell phones and take the next step and sign up for the promotion.

Each message included an alphanumeric code that the customer could present to the Subway cashier (for a free sandwich and a drink) when making a purchase. Expiration dates were instituted for each code, with three to four of them being sent out monthly to customers.

The individual franchisee that came up with the campaign reported that 5,000 customers signed up for the promotion, and that the over 10,000 text messages that were sent out translated into a nearly 9% redemption rate.

According to the company, SMS alerts sent out to the 5,000-plus recipients typically results in "near instant customer traffic." The campaign has since been expanded to other Subway franchises, all of which are looking to cash in on the mobile marketing trend.

15. "Bucking" the Trend.

Ready to help customers celebrate the arrival of summer, Starbucks set-up a "Summer Pursuit" text messaging campaign. It was a trivia quiz that customers participated in by answering three questions, all related to a summer theme. The questions were sent to the customers' cell phones, and those recipients who answered correctly got the opportunity to play Starbucks' "Ultimate Scavenger Hunt" in New York City or Costa Rica.

To play the "Starbucks Summer Pursuit," customers texted the message "SUMMER" to 66268. Within seconds, players received text clues on their mobile phone. The game challenged the novice gamer and excited the enthusiast who had to decipher a series of text message clues. Players were challenged to answer summer and Starbucks-related trivia questions, and then submit them via a mobile phone in the form of a picture or text message.

It was the first mobile scavenger hunt incorporating visual recognition technology to determine whether submitted images represent the correct answer to each question, and also send additional clues to create an ongoing, interactive experience with each player.

The five-week trivia contest/virtual scavenger hunt culminated in a real-time finale in New York City for five lucky contestants (and their guests) chosen at random from those who had registered online.

The hunt for the final clues in the city rewarded the winner (and guest/teammate) with a trip to Costa Rica, one of the world's largest coffee-producing countries. Starbucks has since experimented with other mobile campaigns, and will likely roll out more in the months and years to come.

16. Getting Them Into the Spirit.

Making an age-old brand new and attractive to younger customers is never easy. One international liquor manufacturer has turned to text messaging as a way to create new connections and make its product vogue for 20- to 40-year-old consumers. By reaching out to these consumers on their own terms and in an environment that they're comfortable in (mobile phones), the company has been able to re-establish itself as a desirable brand in a very competitive marketplace.

To draw those customers in, the company developed a series of private liquor tasting events that were invitation-only, and held in six major U.S. metropolitans. Customers had to text a specific keyword (obtained via an email promotion or from the company's website) to a short code to participate. Those who opted in were placed on a VIP list and gained access to the exclusive events.

To enhance its campaign even further, the liquor manufacturer also used a mobile "micro-site" to garner more information (such as how often the company's products were consumed on a monthly and yearly basis) from consumers, who weren't obligated to give up the information.

Just before each event, consumers who opted into the VIP program received special invitations from the company, and information about the featured DJ and types of drinks offered at the exclusive tasting events. Consumers used their mobile phones to RSVP via text message, and then the company sent back text messages that revealed the event's secret location and a password for admittance.

According to the company, every one of those events was sold out. Throughout the campaign, the manufacturer was able to glean important information from its youngest, hippest customers – the ones it was trying to hit harder with the modern marketing approach, and who didn't respond well to traditional advertising methods.

Through the campaign, the company collected over 1,000 opt-in names that it can now contact via mobile marketing with new offers, events and specials.

17. Not Resting on its Laurels.

Kraft Foods may be the #1 food manufacturer in the United States, but that doesn't mean it can rest on its laurels when it comes to keeping its brand in front of new and existing customers.

Not willing to let the mobile marketing trend pass it by, the corporation has used text messaging several times over the last few years, including one campaign designed to put its lesser-known Jacobs instant coffee samples in the hands of its target consumers.

The product sampling campaign was set up to generate market attention and allow users to taste the coffee before buying, while also helping to build a consumer database that it could target with future campaigns. Kraft announced the product line via regional television and print ads, and online banner ads, and used a "text-in" call-to-action system that customers used to make sample requests.

When respondents texted a specific word to a short code, each immediately received an SMS message asking them to text over their names and mailing addresses, or to click on an enclosed link to visit a mobile website to enter the information.

The popular food manufacturer posted success with its campaign, and reported that over 500,000 product samples were mailed out as a result of the efforts. The campaign was continued for three months longer than initially anticipated – a sure sign that it exceeded expectations!

18. Bridging the Gap.

A restaurant's busy lunch hour is usually followed by a lull in the afternoon when everyone gets back to work and starts planning the dinner hour. Chairs and tables sit empty as staffers look for things to do to fill the time.

Looking to fill the void created by this phenomenon, one small franchisee tested out an SMS campaign centered around time-sensitive promotions that would entice diners to visit between 1pm and 5pm on weekdays.

Eager to keep business moving in a positive direction in the afternoon, the restaurants set up a short code system, and used different keywords (for customers to text to those short codes) for each of its locations in order to accurately track consumer responses and habits. And, the individual franchise owners could see who was using their coupons, and at which locations.

At the heart of the promotion was a special coupon redeemable only within certain time frames (1pm to 5pm on weekdays). The promotion was advertised on in-store signs, banners and flyers that were distributed in nearby neighborhoods. The coupons were sent to the mobile phones of recipients who opted into the campaign, and were redeemable at all stores.

Here's how it worked: After responding, customers received a text reply acknowledging their participation in the franchise's VIP program, and offering a certain percentage off of the total bill (more savings for those who "bring a friend") for weekdays between 1pm and 5pm only.

The text messages were sent out once a week, and the company reported a 37% redemption rate and a more than 10% increase in sales for participating locations. Not bad for a few hundred dollars in promotional materials and the time spent preparing the mobile SMS coupons.

19. Brewing up a Mobile Campaign.

A large beer brewer recently implemented a text message marketing promotion that encouraged customers at participating bars to rate their pint of beer via text to vote for a chance to win a prize.

Within three hours of launching the campaign, the company had received over 8,000 entries via text. The popular campaign encouraged entrants to join the company's mobile club and posted less than 2% opt out after its first SMS campaign.

Seems beer drinkers are pretty loyal when it comes to mobile marketing campaigns... especially when there's something in it for them.

Travel and Tourism

20. Traveling the Web.

Airlines, hotels, ground transportation, online travel booking portals and related companies have all embraced text messaging technology as a way to keep in close touch with customers, whether they just wrapped up a trip, are currently on one, or are considering a future vacation. In fact, a recent survey shows that 80% of companies in the travel industry use SMS to communicate with their customers.

As one of the largest online travel booking companies, Orbitz offers alerts via mobile phone, PDA, text message or email. The company can inform customers about flight arrival delays, departure delays, flight cancellations, gate changes and other important events via text message, as long as the customer opts into the service.

Recipients get the important information quickly, and without having to boot up their computers or log into a website. It's right on their phones.

Another online travel portal has discovered that text messaging can also help boost sales. It offers promotional travel offers to its subscribers on a weekly basis, based on individual destination, hotel and travel preferences.

The messages come with an air of "exclusivity" for recipients, who feel that they're being treated to a special deal based on their willingness to opt into the system.

Airlines, hotels and many other entities in the travel industry have used SMS successfully, and are expected to continue doing so over the next few years. You can't really argue with being able to get important travel information on the fly, and being treated to specials and deals that make you feel like a VIP.

21. Premier Treatment.

Already recognized for their "high touch" approaches to customer service, luxury hotels are perfect candidates for targeted text messaging campaigns that cater to discerning recipients. By creating an opt-in list of potential targets for specials, events and announcements, these hotels can quickly and affordably "hit" their best customers, and then receive feedback from them.

One international property recently wanted to let its local customer base know of regular events and promotions that were taking place in the near future, but couldn't figure out a way to do that through traditional marketing channels. After all, direct mail and even email don't always get to their recipients in enough time for the latter to respond in a timely fashion.

But mobile marketing is different, as the hotel found out. It came across the answer to its problem in short, direct text messages sent out just in advance of those events and promotions. Food, beverage and lodging sales could be advertised quickly to the hotel's customer base, which included a high number (roughly 80%) of mobile phone users.

The hotel continues to use text messaging to reach its customer base quickly, while also building its database of recipients who are interested in learning about its specials and upcoming events.

22. Creating VIPs.

The apparel and footwear industries are extremely competitive, with consumers typically shopping for price, convenience and comfort – all of which are being hawked aggressively by today's clothing and shoe sellers. To stand out from the pack, Foot Locker used a text messaging campaign that truly made recipients feel like VIPs.

The company sent out special offers to over 300,000 recipients via its "VIP program," which was tailored for and targeted to AT&T and Verizon Wireless subscribers.

VIP members receive early information on new products, and news about events and special offers. Recipients can control and customize the information on the brands they prefer, thus making the club membership personalized and relevant to every customer.

Through its text messaging program, Foot Locker is able to keep in contact with customers, and keep them up to date with in-store happenings that would otherwise be difficult to communicate in a fast, efficient manner.

When they need footwear, these consumers just might think of Foot Locker first...especially if that brand name has shown up in their SMS inbox in the last few days.

23. Wish They All Could Be California Girls.

With its eye on bronzed, sun-loving California women, a leading swimsuit retail brand turned to SMS text recently to reach its audience. Wanting to increase awareness of a new store that was opening, build brand loyalty among its best customers, and create a list of clients for future marketing opportunities, the company started its mobile push with a text-to-win campaign.

As part of that campaign, the retailer set up a fashion show where the season's hottest swimsuit styles were showcased at an exclusive venue. A text-to-win campaign targeted the 21- to 34-year-old professional women who vied for a free ticket to the event.

The campaign generated over 15% audience participation, and a list of opt-in candidates for future mobile efforts. The word spread about the new store opening, and winners were appreciative of the event that was set up in their honor.

24. Secrets To Their Success.

When a chain of furniture stores on the east coast wanted to increase sales during a slow period last summer, it sent out 6,000 text message coupons to customers who had previously opted in to receive information about special "VIP" offers.

The coupons advertised a "secret sale" that was also promoted via email. According to the retailer, roughly 70% of the money generated from the sale could be traced back to the SMS coupon.

Over $100 in revenue was generated for every dollar that the retailer spent putting together the text message campaign. The results were pretty impressive, and the furniture retailer has used mobile on several other occasions to boost sales.

25. Free Gifts for Participants.

It may be already be a well-known brand for women who want skincare products that rise above and beyond what can be found on discount store shelves, but Estée Lauder also knows that it has to keep up with the times by courting younger, hipper customers.

The company recently introduced a new free Gift Time SMS Text Reminder service which allows customers to sign up to receive text messages to alert them that Gift Time (Estée Lauder's Gift with Purchase offer) is starting at their chosen store.

Available exclusively online, customers can register to receive a text alert via their mobile phone two days before Gift Time starts at their chosen store. Stores presently included in the text message alert service include Boots, Debenhams, Harrods, Harvey Nichols, House of Fraser, John Lewis, and Selfridges.

Estée Lauder was the first cosmetics brand to offer this text message service, and says it's perfect for those customers who have become devoted Gift Time followers.

The text messages are free to sign up for and receive, and are proving an invaluable tool to those who love to be the first to know about special offers. A typical gift will include a mixture of the latest, and best-loved deluxe trial-sized products, along with a handbag and cosmetics pouch. In each gift there is an average of six deluxe trial-sized products including a range of skincare, makeup and fragrances.

The SMS message service ensures loyal customers do not miss out on their exclusive gifts, while providing them with the opportunity to make their skin care, fragrance or makeup purchase at their favorite store.

The SMS messages includes the dates that Gift Time is available to and from, as well as details of the qualifier (if it's with any two Estée Lauder purchases, or any two Estée Lauder purchases, one to be skincare).

26. Catering to Rabid Sports Fans

Fans love free stuff, and sports teams love their fans. These two powerful forces come together to make text messaging a great option for event planners within the sporting industry.

Take the effort initiated a few years ago by the English Cricket Board, which paired up with its team sponsor to create a text-and-win campaign. By texting the answer to a trivia question about a previous cricket match to a short code, fans effectively entered a contest to win an England One Day International shirt.

All correct answers were put into a drawing to win the prize. Fans opted into the promotion hoping to win, and in turn gave the organization another way to reach out to those valued individuals.

Never ones to argue with free stuff that features their favorite team, the cricket fans responded so well to the campaign that the Board set up several other text-and-win contests over the coming years.

27. Getting Them Out of Their Seats.

Fan interaction is an important part of sporting events, and text messaging serves as a prime catalyst for teams that want to get up close and personal with the folks who buy seats in their venues.

One NBA team looking to encourage participation at it games and develop an opt-in list for future promotions turned to a simple SMS campaign to get the job done.

Using a short code and text-to-win campaign, the team tested out a few ways to get fans involved. It found the best success with a trivia game that awarded winning recipients with autographed team memorabilia.

Along with the chances to win great stuff, the team also offered a schedule of regular announcements via text that the fans came to expect, and appreciate, along with SMS offers for discounted ticket prices.

The effort didn't start and stop in the arena. By extending the campaign to the actual, televised games, the team was able to involve "at home" fans with trivia questions and other fun, interactive games.

The extra push increased the NBA team's opt-in list exponentially, and also boosted ticket sales by 610 additional units the first season the campaign was implemented (all in return for an investment of about $1,300).

28. Spreading the Word.

Fans aren't the only ones who need information quickly about sporting events. Volunteers and participants also need the 411. The Greater Washington Sports Alliance recently rolled out a mobile messaging service for its SunTrust National Marathon in Washington, D.C.

The marathon joined the Marine Corps Marathon as one of several national races that used a message alerting service to connect with runners, fans and others.

The campaign allowed it to reach several different audiences over the weekend's event, including volunteers, runners, spectators, local-community (residents, businesses, etc.), and as a secondary way to communicate among internal staff, operations units and medical personnel.

Sign up information was posted on the race website, as well as in newsletters, email messaging, training documents, event signage, and the official Spectator Guide.

As the event grows, the coordinator says, "It is critical to be able to develop a communications plan that will allow us to reach out to the masses instantly."

Expect to see more amateur events relying on SMS text to get the word out quickly to everyone who is involved. For just a few minutes of time and pennies in monetary investment, SMS is the perfect solution for these types of events.

29. Music to Their Ears.

When a concert promoter wanted to measure the effectiveness of its ongoing billboard advertising and build a database of mobile subscribers, it decided that an SMS text campaign would fit the bill perfectly.

The 4-month-long campaign was based on a short code and keywords like "BLING" and "POP," depending on the specific call to action.

The campaign targeted tourists and residents in a specific region, and was based on unique keywords that were posted on five billboards, and coupons placed in outgoing text messages, in order to measure location effectiveness.

Drivers reading the billboards could text one of several keywords to the company's short code and receive a special offer, and a prompt to purchase tickets for upcoming events. Phrases like, "Buy Now" and "Last Chance Offer," were used to entice customers to place ticket orders immediately.

The campaign exceeded expectations for the company, which built its subscriber database to over 1,500 members (and continues to expand it with additional SMS campaigns). Combined, the five billboards returned a 16% conversion rate for all opt-in respondents, and resulted in a more than 1,000% return on initial investment for the company.

Not only did the event coordinator get a solid base of subscribers for future mobile campaigns, but it was also able to get a solid gauge on its billboard advertising – a medium that was previously impossible to measure and track.

30. Personality Counts.

A veteran of the radio waves, Rick Dees is one DJ who has tapped into the power of mobile advertising several times over the last few years. Most recently, Dees & The Weekly Top 40 Countdown rolled out a "text to win a laptop" campaign with the goal of increasing the number of listeners who interacted with its Friday and Sunday Top 40 Countdown shows.

The company also wanted to grow its database of opt-in subscribers. To make that happen, it created a text to win mobile campaign that was recorded for radio play and distributed to a nationwide audience via the Rick Dees syndicated network of stations.

The mobile campaign was a success. Over 10,000 text messages were generated over a 3-day period, and about 6,000 unique mobile numbers opted into the campaign, which offered a free laptop to the winner of the contest.

The winner walked away happy, and the syndicated radio show came away with an impressive number of fans to target with future campaigns. It was a win-win all the way around.

Telecommunications

31. Phoning Home.

The mobile phone companies themselves are also cashing in on the text-messaging trend. A Canadian firm used a $1,000 "text and win" promotion to help build business.

Customers texted the word "TRIVIA" to a specific short code, and in doing so gained a single chance to win the $1,000 prize.

Every month, the mobile carrier would select one winner from the many entries received during the prior 30 days. Winners walked away with the bounty, while the company itself increased its database with customers eager to win the $1,000 in a future month.

32. "Smacking" Them Down.

Professional wrestling is known for its extreme antics, eye-catching advertisements and spectacular matches. It's pretty hard to ignore, as fans found out recently when World Wrestling Entertainment (WWE) rolled out a live sweepstakes via text message.

The one-week campaign used a short code and the keyword "WWE" to entice communications between the company and its subscribers. Respondents had the chance to win four tickets to a WWE Smackdown Live show.

The text messages were sent to a subscriber base (which was owned by the wireless carrier that ran the campaign), and alerted those individuals to the contest and told them to how to enter it (by texting the keyword to the short code). The campaign was advertised at the mobile carrier's locations, and also on a Facebook page and website.

The carrier reports that just under 10% of all subscribers texted in to join, and that it intends to run more subscriber sweepstakes in the future. Guess you can call this one a successful tag-team approach to mobile marketing!

Automotive

33. At Your Service.

You wouldn't necessarily associate a quick oil change center with cutting-edge marketing tactics, but at least one franchisee is paving its way in the SMS marketing arena.

Unsatisfied with the results of its email and direct mail campaigns designed to get new customers in the door, the oil change center tested out a combination of text message reminders and coupons for about six months in 2010.

Utilizing keywords and a short code, the company was able to study and measure the effectiveness of SMS oil change reminders and coupons, compared to its previous marketing efforts.

The company used customer handout cards that explained how to opt-into the campaign by texting a vehicle's license plate number to the short code. Customers could also opt-in by visiting a dedicated website.

The franchisee was able to identify customers and the communication channel they preferred, be it text, email or direct mail. From there, it set up an SMS, email or mail postcard system of reminders that would be sent to the customer with a coupon for a discounted oil change.

The campaign paid off. According to the company, 32% of customers (just over 2,000 out of a total of 6,800) who came in for service opted-in to receive future oil change reminders by text message.

Another 500+ customers requested future email reminders, bringing the total number of customers who visited and chose to receive text and/or email reminders instead of mailed reminders to over 40%.

On average, 21% of customers who received a mailed postcard reminder returned for service within 45 days, with email performing better with 29% of customers returning for service. The company has adopted a full-time short code campaign and discontinued its mail reminders.

34. The High-Touch Approach.

Auto manufacturers have also caught mobile fever. Audi, for example, recently gave auto show attendees the ability to receive electronic brochures of its 2011 lineup by delivering the content instantly to their mobile phones as an alternative to printed copies.

The program officially launched during public days at the North American International Auto Show in Detroit, and is part of the automaker's increased focus on environmental awareness.

In fact, the company says that the move to digital distribution is expected to reduce the amount of printed material handed out at shows by up to 90% by the end of its first season of use.

The campaign is also expected to have a considerable impact on the printing, shipping and distribution costs associated with delivering brochures to millions of attendees over the course of the auto show season.

Audi's campaign enables visitors with smartphones to scan special, 2-dimensional "QR" barcodes that have been placed next to each model on the show floor. Scanning a code adds that model's brochure to an online library that can be viewed right from a phone, or from any computer after the show.

Visitors without smartphones can send free SMS text messages to populate their libraries- so anyone capable of sending a text can make use of the platform. The service is complimentary, requires no pre-registration, and visitors' personal information is never revealed. The effort has paid off so far, as evidenced by the fact that Audi will continue to offer this service at major auto shows throughout the rest of the 2010-2011 season in the U.S.

35. Vroom, Vroom

Harley-Davidson is a venerable American brand that few people *wouldn't* immediately recognize, but that doesn't mean the company can afford to sit back and wait for customers to come into the doors of its retail locations.

Two Harley-Davidson dealerships recently took a more proactive approach and launched an SMS campaign designed to provoke and maintain communications with its most loyal customers.

The campaign rolled out in January 2010, and has been in force ever since. At its core is the goal of expanding the popular brand of motorcycles to reach a new demographic, while at the same time opening communication lines with existing customers and letting them know about special events and sales at the dealerships.

Using an SMS campaign and other mobile marketing tactics, the dealerships were able to increase both sales and customer visits to each store (through "VIP" mobile clubs, for example). New and existing customers were both invited to opt into the VIP club, and were targeted via a mobile marketing campaign and a social media effort.

Through the campaign, customers received updates via text regarding events, sales and VIP-only deals. They also get special, insider information about "Bike Night" locations, and other off-site events sponsored by the company.

More specifically, one of the locations increased its opt-in list of subscribers with a "Ten Days of Christmas" promotion that found the store giving away a $100 gift card daily to a lucky subscriber.

To say the Harley-Davidson dealerships were satisfied with the results of their mobile efforts would be an understatement. According to the owners, each location was able to increase its geographic and demographic reach to new levels, and also build a database of loyal, interested customers.

Each location tracked impressive growth through their respective mobile marketing campaigns, and reported a "tremendous response" almost immediately following the delivery of mobile alerts announcing sales and other special events.

The campaigns went – and, continue to go – a long way in helping to further solidify an age-old, recognizable brand in the minds of consumers.

36. In and Out in a Jiffy

Jiffy Lube is another automotive brand that has jumped feet first into the mobile marketing waters. Bent on becoming "the" oil change specialist for younger generations of drivers that had yet to have the company's brand emblazoned in its brains, the company knew the traditional Yellow Pages and word-of-mouth wasn't going to cut it in today's competitive business environment.

What the 2,000-location company needed was a new, innovative way to reach its younger customer base. It found what it was looking for in a mobile marketing campaign that hit cell phone users in new ways that the company's traditional marketing could not.

The company launched its campaign in Los Angeles, where residents spend a lot of time behind the wheels of their cars, commuting to and from work, and stuck in traffic. With cell phones close by, those drivers were perfect candidates for Jiffy Lube's SMS text campaign.

That campaign featured coupons for discounted oil changes, and was advertised using text alerts that were delivered through online news sites. One offer featured a 20 percent off coupon while another was based on a specific dollar cost savings off of an oil change. Separate keywords were used to measure response, and were used in tandem with a short code that users dialed on their cell phones to take advantage of the offers.

Concurrently, Jiffy Lube was running a similar campaign via its website, and using that online presence to prompt users to "text in" and get a coupon to use at their next service visit.

All respondents received a text message that included a coupon redemption code, and details about the special offer. They were also encouraged to text in one more time and submit their zip codes to receive specific information about the nearest Jiffy Lube automotive shops.

According to the company, the mobile marketing campaign was successful, and even did better than the companion website campaign that was set up. Jiffy Lube reports that over 25% of recipients texted in their zip codes and received a list of "closest" stores, thus giving the company an idea of exactly where its most loyal customer base is located.

Over 200 SMS coupons were redeemed at company locations, representing about 10% of the respondents that they were sent to. And while the "percent off" coupon generated more response, the "dollars off" version actually brought more customers in the door to get their special offers.

37. Putting Them in the "Hotseat."

At Purdue University, professors who are teaching in large lecture halls have embraced SMS as an instructional aid. Using an application developed on campus, the educators who enrolled in the program have come to think of social networking via texting and online portals as a tool, rather than a distraction.

Known as "Hotseat," the application allows students to comment on the class, and then enables other participants – including professors, students and teaching assistants – to view those messages.

Students either use their Twitter, Facebook or MySpace accounts to post the messages, or they log into the Hotseat website to send text messages. The application resides on the web, so there is no software for professors or students to install.

Created by a team of developers on campus, the system was intended as a way to manage the logistics of teaching a classroom of 100-plus students. "We were looking for a better way for students to engage the instructor and each other in terms of classroom discussion," said one of the developers, "and to find a way to encourage that type of interaction both in and out of the classroom."

Purdue University launched three Hotseat pilot courses (with two different faculty members) for the fall semester. So far, feedback has been largely positive, with professors using the application in myriad ways.

A faculty advisor, for example, will give a short lecture, retreat to his computer for a few minutes to address the questions and concerns raised by students via text, and then recommence lecturing. It's a seamless process that far surpasses any traditional method, particularly when it comes to teaching lecture halls that are packed with hundreds of college students.

38. SMS as a College Outreach Tool.

Like many colleges, the University of Louisville was struggling with a major student recruitment challenge:

how to effectively communicate with thousands of prospective students, and also keep in close contact with an additional 2,500 incoming freshmen.

The task was daunting, and found the admissions office scrambling to communicate with a broad range of students who needed to be in the loop on campus events, orientation activities and special programs.

The university needed a solution that would allow it to quickly and conveniently contact all of its incoming students. Knowing that a large percentage of that target audience carried cell phones, the college decided that a mobile campaign would be a great way to alleviate some of the stress that its admissions and recruiting teams were feeling.

The school began using a system of text message blasts sent out to about 500 incoming freshman who opted-in to receive the pertinent information that they weren't otherwise receiving (namely because so few of them actually checked email or snail mail on a regular basis).

One text message campaign offered incoming freshman a week of free campus parking if they responded with a text citing the three things that they were most looking forward to during the upcoming school year.

The strategy has been so successful that the university now uses SMS text to keep in touch with all prospective students, informing them about campus visits, events, application deadlines and other important points.

In the future, Louisville plans to use text to reach out to prospective students with information on campus visits, application deadlines and more. The return on investment has been high for the school, whose admissions team takes just a few minutes to type up and send out the messages.

Using an SMS campaign, The University of Louisville has found a very effective way to reach its young, cell phone-toting audience with important information about their college educations. Without this cutting-edge mobile campaign, most of the communications would have fallen by the wayside, leaving both students and administrators in the lurch.

Financial Services

39. Dollars and Cents.

People like to be kept in their loop about their financial statuses, which puts the banks of the world in the perfect position to use SMS alerts and text campaigns to keep their customers informed and up to date. Nasty surprises that come weeks after the fact via mail are never welcome, and are particularly onerous when they involve money.

One overseas bank recently became the first in its country to use SMS as a customer communication method. Using SMS alerts, the institution has been able to keep those clients informed and up to speed about their account transactions.

Using the system, any type of fraud or error can be caught and mediated quickly. This is a far cry from the old fashioned, snail mail method that puts consumers in a bind by not making them aware of problems until days or weeks after they occur.

The ongoing text campaign finds the bank notifying its customers immediately about account transactions via SMS messages that are delivered right to their cell phones. Those customers must voluntarily opt into the system, which has seen widespread adoption due to its expediency and accuracy of delivering important, financial information.

The campaign allows customers to basically stay up to the minute with any and all activity taking place in their accounts, whether they're using just a basic savings account, or a more complex web of savings, checking and investment options.

The system has gone a long way in reducing fraud, according to the bank, and has also resulted in higher customer retention rates. Customer trust in the system is high due to the fact that accurate, useful text messages are delivered nearly 100% of the time.

When it comes to protecting their assets, customers are more than happy to opt into SMS text systems that virtually ensure that the information is delivered on time, every time.

40. Not Your Average Insurance Salesman.

One short-term insurer that markets its products via a traditional broker network has come under pressure from new entrants, offering to cut traditional premium rates by selling direct.

To compete effectively, the company decided it had to offer an exceptionally high level of service to its customers, in order to retain their loyalty and their business.

The insurer saw rapid, consistent communications with those clients as a key component of this strategy.

The company launched an SMS alert service for its brokers and clients, and used the campaign to keep those individuals apprised of the progress made on any claims.

For example, a customer who is involved in a car accident will typically register a claim via the company's 24/7 contact center. The claim is confirmed immediately to the customer via SMS, along with a reference number and a contact number for further inquiries.

Both the customer and the assessor are notified of the assessment details via SMS, and the customer is alerted once more when the claim has been accepted.

Within a year of launching the service, the insurance company grew its SMS campaign from 5,000 messages a month, to 25,000 messages a month. It continues to use and expand its mobile marketing strategy, knowing that it's the fastest, easiest way to keep its constituents in the loop on important information and data.

41. Pressing Tax Matters…Solved!

As the world's preeminent tax services provider, H&R Block understands all too well that tax season is, for many, a time of dread, uncertainty and overall confusion. That's why it has repeatedly turned to SMS as a way to disseminate tax-related answers combined with advertising about the company's Free Online Tax Prep service.

The program not only provides H&R Block with another connection point to consumers at a critical time of the year, but also provides consumers with easy access to much-needed free answers to their difficult tax questions. And, as an added benefit, taxpayers can also learn about H&R Block's Free Tax Prep service on the go, from their mobile devices.

H&R Block's SMS ads ran in tandem with additional online advertising initiatives. Upon making tax-related inquiries, users received SMS ads from H&R Block, promoting and directing users to a website where they could learn more about H&R Block's Free Online Tax Prep service.

H&R Block has used myriad mobile campaigns over the last few years, and will presumably continue to do so as mobs of stressed-out taxpayers look for relief from their tax woes.

Charities and Emergency Organizations

42. Coming to Their Aid.

If the world's natural disasters are any indication, text messaging is a great way to motivate masses of people to open up their wallets and donate to those in need. The earthquakes in Haiti are just one example of how well this system works.

Within just a few weeks of setting up its text campaign, the Red Cross had already raised more than $800,000 for Haiti through their $10 text message donation initiative (text "Haiti" to 90999), which was backed by the United States State Department. Anyone wishing to help the cause could text "Haiti" to 90999 to send a $10 donation to the Red Cross.

According to the Red Cross, "Raising this amount of money, $10 at time, is a true testament to the American spirit." Credit the organization with making that happen. It not only set up the simplest, most state-of-the-art donation method possible, but it also rounded out its efforts with a social media presence and outreach.

43. Red Alert!

The power of SMS is often experienced during situations that attract nationwide and even worldwide attention. Most recently, this was reinforced during the tragic events at Virginia Tech University, where shootings left a number of students and teachers injured and dead.

Because of the overwhelming amount of cellular call attempts, the cellular voice networks became congested and blocked many calls from going through during this emergency.

While the voice calls could not get through, SMS text messages were sent. The reason SMS text messaging is more reliable during disaster situations is that the cellular carriers use a different network for SMS text messaging than they do for voice traffic. If the voice channels become overwhelmed, the text-messaging network can still function.

44. Averting Disaster.

Text messaging can help emergency teams mobilize quickly and avert disaster. Parts of the Gulf Coast, for example, were much better prepared during Hurricane Gustav, a Category 2 hurricane that struck Louisiana a few years after Hurricane Katrina ripped through the same area, causing massive damage and destruction.

Several state and local governments in the Gulf Coast region issued multimodal emergency notifications to keep people informed before, during and after Hurricane Gustav.

In coordination with other actions, these timely alerts kept emergency responders informed while simultaneously keeping the general public out of harm's way.

The City of Brandon, Mississippi used the SMS text alert system three days before Hurricane Gustav to issue warnings and precautions. It turned to the system again during and after Gustav to update first responders as events developed. By the time the storm had passed, multiple tornado warnings had been issued, allowing those first responders to adequately prepare for the worst.

This is just one example of how life and limb can be spared with a targeted, fast mobile marketing campaign.

Miscellaneous

45. Meet the Prez.

One of the best examples of SMS in action can be seen in a very public place: the White House. There, President Barack Obama has proven that he is a tech-savvy politician who knows how to motivate the masses through their mobile phones.

The examples of the President's mobile campaigns over the last few years are many and varied in nature, but one that stands out was actually launched before he was even sworn into office. It was then that he announced his choice of vice presidential running mate not at a press conference nor on national television, but via text message.

Unlike his opponent Senator John McCain, who openly admitted that he didn't have a clue about how to use a computer, let alone orchestrate a text message campaign, President-elect Obama caught the eye of young voters who were ready for a change.

In a text message and e-mail campaign, Obama's campaign team alerted anyone who would listen that the candidate would announce his VP choice sometime before the Democratic National Convention through a text message to his supporters.

To get on the distribution list, individuals had to text the message "VP" to the Obama SMS short code number, 62262. The campaign also allowed people to sign up for an email alert on Obama's website, and/or receive notice through Twitter (yet another favorite means of communication for the President).

By using a mobile campaign to alert supporters of his VP selection, Obama not only effectively controlled the message he sent out, but he also distributed it directly to hundreds of thousands (if not millions) of individuals who opted into the SMS campaign. In the end, the President wound up with important data about his supporters – many of whom could be hit up for campaign contributions at a later date – while positioning himself as a candidate who isn't afraid to use technology to connect with them.

46. Spreading the Good Word.

AskMoses.com, the world's leading website for Jewish information and the only one offering live chat services with scholars 24 hours-a-day, 6 days a week, recently launched SMS text messaging to deliver content directly to mobile phones.

AskMoses.com has consistently been at the forefront of Jewish Internet innovation, providing live communication via chat messaging to millions of visitors each year.

Now, in addition to its live chats and vast online information knowledgebase, the site can send Jewish-oriented content and Sabbath and Holiday reminders to users' cell phones and handheld devices.

"We're the first Jewish website to offer these services to the public," said Rabbi Simcha Backman, Director of AskMoses.com. "We decided to take the AskMoses.com experience mobile to make it available anywhere, anytime."

AskMoses.com offers detailed information about Judaism and lets visitors receive anonymous, live assistance from Jewish scholars who are available 24 hours a day, six days a week. Since the site's founding, its scholars have held millions of live chat sessions, answered hundreds of thousands of e-mails, and written thousands of essays.

Along the way, they have helped people with everything from simple questions on Jewish holiday customs and researching school reports to complex life challenges like troubled marriages and suicide attempts.

The explosive popularity of handheld mobile devices presented a new avenue for AskMoses to disseminate Jewish information. With young people increasingly using SMS text messaging to communicate, the website's creators felt it imperative to offer services geared toward that segment of the population to complement their already popular live chat experience.

"Keeping a website at the cutting edge of technology requires ingenuity," said Rabbi Backman, adding that AskMoses.com's next step will be to offer a live chat module for handheld devices.

47. Welcoming Them Into the World.

Keystone Mercy Health Plan, the largest Medicaid managed care organization in Pennsylvania, recently partnered with The Maternity Care Coalition and the Healthy Mothers, Healthy Babies (HMHB) Coalition, to launch the Philadelphia text4baby campaign.

Keystone Mercy launched the campaign to educate and encourage the use of the service to its Wee Care prenatal program members. Text4baby is a free, mobile information service designed to promote maternal and child health by providing pregnant women and new moms with detailed health tips, via

SMS text message, to assist them in caring for themselves and their children.

The program, which was launched nationwide in February 2010, has nearly 35,000 enrollees, including 1,042 participants in Pennsylvania.

Women sign up for the free service by texting "BABY" (or "BEBE," in Spanish) to 511411. Each woman receives three, SMS text messages every week, timed to their due date or baby's age, up to the child's first birthday. Messages include subject matter geared toward nutrition, immunizations, labor and delivery, car seat safety, breastfeeding and mental health.

The insurer plans to promote the initiative among its more than 5,000 Wee Care prenatal program participants. The company also uses SMS text messaging to provide information to diabetics, smokers and to people with weight-management issues.

Under each category, SMS technology has improved the health of its participants. For example, 28% of smokers receiving SMS messages quit smoking, as compared to 13% of the control group. It's pretty hard to beat results like that.

48. In the City.

Birmingham City Council in the U.K., began using SMS messaging a few years ago to provide local residents with the option to instantly enter its latest competition. By implementing the SMS solution for a recent street naming competition, Birmingham City Council has been able to reach a wide audience and as a result has seen a greater uptake in entrants.

An important part of Birmingham City Council's mission is to communicate effectively with the public and ensure local community involvement in local projects. "We run a number of campaigns throughout the year to enable the local community to have an active involvement in the development of Birmingham," said a city spokesperson.

It's most recent campaign centered on providing citizens with the opportunity to suggest street names for a new development within the city. The selected names were then allocated to contractors, and gave residents the opportunity to contribute to local landmarks.

The city has been able to move away from previous campaign activities such as direct mail and leaflet drops, which are expensive to produce and require a lot of resource, and focus on providing a text messaging facility instead. In order to raise awareness of the campaign and the new text facility, it included the short-code number on posters around the city, to inform residents of how they can easily submit their entries via SMS.

Residents sent text messages to a short code wherever they saw the poster. Throughout the campaign, the city saw a greater level of participation in the competition and has been commended as one of the council's most successful campaigns, in terms of participation, to date.

Ready, Set, Go!

You've seen how text messaging works and learned a great deal about how companies are using it to reach customers, obtain critical data about those individuals, beef up their opt-in databases and positions themselves as forward-thinking organizations that aren't afraid to try new marketing ideas.

Now it's your turn. Using the information you've learned in this chapter – and the mobile ad, social media, proximity marketing, QR code and mobile app advice and examples that you'll read about in upcoming chapters – you'll be ready to launch an SMS text campaign that blends well with your existing advertising efforts.

In fact, this affordable, easy and fast method of spreading the word and connecting with customers may even replace some of the more expensive and cumbersome tactics you've used since the dawn of time.

In the resource section of this book you'll find a list of trusted providers that we carefully selected and included for your convenience. Check out these options as you prepare your own text messaging campaign, and be sure to interview and research any partners that you chose to work with.

In the next chapter we'll look at some different types of mobile campaigns that fall under the "mobile ad" umbrella. Flip to the next page to get started...

Mobile Ads

Text messaging may be a popular activity for most cell phone users—and a good way to reach a mobile audience via short, text-based messages – but mobile advertising goes beyond SMS to include more sophisticated ads. In the rest of this book we'll look closely at a few other viable options for small businesses looking to cash in on the mobile advertising trend, starting with mobile ads.

Unlike basis SMS, mobile advertising incorporates the ability to offer a call to action or brand banner within the mobile application, whether it's mobile web (WAP), text messaging, pictures (MMS), or video. At its simplest, mobile advertising is the practice of placing a marketing message, promotion or sponsorship call-to-action within various media properties that make up the mobile channel, including mobile web, search, applications, text messaging, multimedia messaging, email voice, Bluetooth and content.

Costs for such ads vary according to the time and effort that is put into the ad itself (from the self-made, low-budget production to a sophisticated spot that's produced by a professional) and the delivery method. A common approach is to use ad units that include text links that are embedded in graphical banner and display ads. The text links are usually sold on a cost per click (CPC) basis, and provide an excellent way to measure ROI for your campaigns. The results are easy to track, and make it possible for you to adjust your campaign to achieve your ROI goals.

Mobile ads are effective. In fact, digital marketing research firm InsightExpress reports that mobile ads perform around five times better than Internet ad placements. The study measured unaided awareness, aided awareness, ad awareness, message association, brand favorability and purchase intent, and included a comparison of mobile media types and verticals to the effect of online advertising.

These findings continue to show the power of mobile as an advertising channel. "Mobile continues to prove that it is an effective advertising medium," said a company spokesperson. "Now, when we're able to look at performance by the type of mobile advertising technology, we understand the strength even more."

A Powerful Medium

Mobile ads can be standalone, or they can be produced in conjunction with a banner ad that, for example, is featured directly below the banner itself (thus making the ad more eye-catching). These types of ads allow you to highlight your call to action without taking away from the visual appeal of the banner itself.

The ads themselves are communicated to the consumer/target via a handset. These ads are most commonly seen as a Mobile Web Banner (top of page), Mobile Web Poster (bottom of page banner), and full screen, which appear while a requested mobile web page is "loading." Other forms of this type of advertising are SMS and MMS ads, mobile gaming ads and mobile video ads (pre, mid and post roll).

These banner and display ads are sold on a CPC and CPM (cost per 1000 impressions) basis. To stand out, they can incorporate video and/or animation (but not all handsets are capable of receiving and displaying these types of moving ads yet, so proceed with caution if you're using a graphics-heavy campaign).

The mobile ad space presents significant opportunity for small businesses. According to the MMA, the mobile space encompassing smartphones and tablet PCs is expected to continue to grow at a steady clip as advertisers jump on the opportunity to reach consumers right in their pockets or purses. Another research firm, The Kelsey Group projects a $3.1 billion dollar market by 2013.

Nuts and Bolts

The mobile advertising landscape is still somewhat of a Wild, Wild West for companies looking to tap into this growing medium. For example, there are more than 5,000 different types of handsets available, so no one banner size is optimal for all. Although the MMA is working with wireless carriers to increase standardization, there are still key differences in how the various browsers display ads and how users view and click on them. This is something that you will want to take into consideration when you are developing your own mobile ad campaign.

Of course, our philosophy is that the best way to learn about new marketing terrain is by listening to the stories of those who have been there. As you already read in the last chapter, this book is filled with case studies that show how other companies are already successfully using one or more mobile marketing methods.

In this chapter, we'll start by giving you a few examples of mobile ads in action. Through these case studies, you'll see how other businesses are using mobile ads to sell products and services to build brand awareness and cultivate robust mobile databases that can be used for future campaigns.

Just like last time, we've grouped the examples by industry so that you can quickly locate those that best relate to your own needs, although we encourage you to read through all of them as each has its own nuances and nuggets of advice to share.

49. Morning Java Break.

Finding true "morning people" isn't always easy to do, particularly in today's overstressed, overtaxed society. Undaunted by the challenge, Seattle's Best Coffee decided to help its customers "Discover Their Inner Morning Person," by using a mobile ad campaign for a new, canned iced coffee beverage.

The goal was to promote the beverages to select markets on the West Coast via an engaging and targeted cross platform campaign. The coffeehouse was primarily looking to reach adults over the age of 30, which is a demographic consistent with the audience of smartphone users, to drive awareness and trial of an exciting and delicious new beverage.

Seattle's Best developed a variety of mobile ad units and an interactive website landing experience that was compatible with thousands of mobile devices, thus making the mobile ad campaign pretty much ubiquitous for its audience. The campaign included standard banner ads placed in strategic locations online and animated multi-panel banners with text links.

The company also took out full-page ads (or, interstitials) on iPhones and iPads, with expandable banners that could run on both the Apple and Android platforms.

Seattle's Best reported excellent results from its multi-faceted campaign. Nearly 140,000 users found their way to the company's mobile site as a result of its ads, and the full-page ads posted an interaction rate of more than 5.5%. The phone interstitials recorded a click-through rate of 5.4, and the company's CPM ad placements averaged a CTR of nearly 1%.

Not bad results for a campaign targeting an elusive group of individuals who would probably rather ignore their inner morning person, hoping that he or she will go away and let them sleep.

Retail and Apparel

50. Putting Shoes on Their Feet.

Consumers don't always discern between the major athletic shoe brands, and that's why maintaining high brand awareness among those buyers is of utmost importance to companies like Adidas. With young, urbanites on its radar screen, the company launched a mobile ad campaign designed to engage that target audience and get it thinking about the company's shoes.

The company's overall goals included building brand awareness while also developing brand associations with its "Superstar" brand. The basketball shoe has been manufactured by Adidas since 1969, and was released as a low top version of the Pro Model basketball shoe.

Nicknamed the "shell toe," "shell shoes," and "shell tops" for their rubber shell toe piece, their iconic design is known as one of the major influences in the sneaker culture. (Think Run DMC, and the group's recognizable black-and-white Adidas sneakers, which they even sang about in one of their hits.)

From the mobile ad campaign, Adidas also wanted to drive traffic to its mobile site, get people to watch the videos on that site, and download ringtones and wallpaper. To make that happen, the company ran graphical banner ads and text link ads aimed at college students and users of its mobile service provider's network.

Concurrently, graphical banner ads and text link ads drove traffic to the Adidas Originals mobile website, where they could select their favorite type of music and listen to sample tracks from up-and-coming artists in each genre. Listeners were able to download ringtones from their favorite musicians, watch video performances, opt-in to receive more ringtones in the future, send their friends ringtones, and even enter their zip code to find the nearest location where they could purchase Adidas Superstars.

According to the company, the campaign drove over 200,000 visitors to the Adidas Originals mobile website where each visitor posted more than 2.9 page views. Visitors downloaded over 100,000 ringtones, and over 10,000 of them forwarded those ringtones to friends.

Based on those results, it looks like Adidas has found an inexpensive and efficient way to stand out in the crowded athletic shoe and apparel industry.

51. The Flowers are in Bloom.

Wanting to enable flower and gift purchases for consumers who are on the go while also driving mobile traffic to its website, a major online delivery service recently used a mobile ad campaign to meet those goals while also increasing click-through rates (CTRs) and conversions.

To achieve those goals, the online merchant began delivering ads to customers who were searching from their mobile devices. And to help customers order flowers and gifts on the go, the company launched a mobile site where shoppers can log on to the site, browse through a number of popular flower selections, and complete purchases from a mobile device.

Through the company's mobile site, customers can order same-day delivery, right from their mobile devices. The online retailer also began using Ad Mob ads to target this large and growing audience and drive prospects to the company's mobile site.

Based on the success of those standard mobile ads, the company also opted in some of its desktop-based campaigns to show on iPhones and Android devices, as well as other mobile devices with full (HTML) Internet browsers.

The online retailer was pleased with the results of its mobile ad campaign. It received over 2 million mobile impressions since launching the initiative, and was able to increase traffic and incremental orders. The company also boosted click-through rates and conversions, achieving CTRs that were two to three times higher on mobile than on its desktop-based, pay-per-click campaigns.

Other benefits included customer convenience, thanks to the mobile ordering site, and a leg up on the competition that was just beginning to explore mobile marketing options.

52. High Fashion Goes Mobile.

Armani Exchange created a mobile website for its spring 2009 collection. The website was built for the iPhone since those users were the right target customers for their fashion--18-49 years old, higher income and tech savvy.

To support the launch, Armani used a mobile advertising campaign with the objectives of increasing awareness, opt-ins, and building a stronger connection to their brand. The mobile ads included iPhone banner and text ads targeting Entertainment, Lifestyle and Music audiences.

The results of their mobile effort:
- 48,000 users to their mobile website
- 36,000 video views
- 2,600 store locator look-ups
- Average click through rate (CTR): 1.22%
- Interaction rates as high as 14.5% on the mobile site

It should be noted that your click-through rates on mobile ads tend to be higher than with the same ad on Google AdWords. In this example, a 1.22% CTR is excellent as an AdWords effort would probably be half of that percentage or lower.

When it comes to mobile advertising, you will find the following tends to be true:

- Click through rate is higher
- Cost per click price is lower
- The speed at which your budget is spent is faster

When you plan your mobile advertising campaign, it is important to set your daily spending limits, and to test your ads before increasing your spending.

53. Stella!

Stella McCartney entered the mobile marketing arena with a campaign to introduce the company's spring and summer 2009 collections. The objective: to build awareness and interest using mobile banner ads and a mobile website.

The mobile website was an interactive experience that mirrored window shopping on a mobile phone via a series of "local looks" that showcased all of the items in the collection. The site included a mobile store locator and an opt-in for news and updates from the brand.

Publishing

54. Not For Dummies.

As part of a traditional media plan, Wiley Publishing decided to add a mobile component to promote their Books for Dummies. Using mobile text ads Wiley offered consumers $5.00 off any Dummies Book. In addition, consumers were encouraged to come and visit the mobile website and opt-in for any future offers.

The results were that the mobile ads had a 1.4% click through rate, which was four times higher than their normal online rate. The opt-ins rate was excellent as well at 34%.

55. A Slam Dunk Win.

Penguin Books promoted Nick Hornby's novel, *Slam*, using mobile text ads at a targeted in-house list. The promotion offered a 90 second audio download of the book's first chapter. Incredibly, 67% of the list visited the mobile landing page, and 51% of those respondents downloaded the audio clip.

Sports and Entertainment

56. I Want My MTV!

A television network is only as good as the people who run it and produce the shows that appear on its airwaves. Wanting to reach an audience of hip, European digital artists, Viacom Brand Solutions International (the parent company of MTV) launched a mobile ad campaign specifically targeting this demographic

The 6-week-long "Engine Room" series provided four competing teams of digital artists with the chance to show off their design skills. As part of the series, MTV ran a campaign to drive those young, creative, design-savvy mobile users in key European markets to the show's mobile website to participate in an HP notebook design contest.

The mobile ad campaign invited prospects to submit designs online and register for a chance to win a special edition notebook featuring their own design on the cover. Participants could also view and assess the entire gallery of design submissions.

To help drive traffic throughout various European markets via mobile ads, MTV partnered with a leading mobile advertising network. According to the company, the iPhone proved to be an especially responsive medium due to the provider's iPhone ad unit, which was specifically created to enhance the user experience and increase response rates.

MTV used its provider's mobile ad platform to run display banners and local language text link ads to country-specific mobile sites for the United Kingdom, Spain, France, Germany, Italy and the Netherlands. When a consumer clicked on one of the ads, MTV's landing pages encouraged them to submit design ideas, vote on design submissions and compete to win prizes.

The mobile campaign delivered strong results for MTV, which recorded average click-through-rates (CTR) of 1.2% on iPhones in the UK and an average CTR across all six markets that exceeded 0.90%. These rates may not seem high when compared to more traditional marketing methods, but in reality they are quite impressive in light of the number of potential users that MTV was targeting via the mobile ad campaign.

Over the 6-week-long campaign MTV reported more than 11 million ad impressions and exceeded its campaign objectives in terms of clicks.

57. I Want My MTV Award Show!

To promote the MTV Music Awards in Europe, MTV ran targeted text ads with messages to get their audience involved with the upcoming show. There were a series of cost per click ads that gave people many different reasons to click on the text and visit their site. The messages including getting the inside scoop from the show and free videos.

The results were excellent with a 300% increase in traffic and a 400% increase in downloads.

58. Call Kevin Garnett.

The first mobile web ads that I noticed were for Adidas ringtones and wallpapers. They were used when the company decided to test mobile advertising to capture opt-in emails using its "Basketball is Brotherhood" campaign.

Using Kevin Garnett (KG), the Boston Celtics basketball all-star, Adidas conducted a "click to call KG" campaign with an opt-in email. The opt-in request was made by mobile phone, with the user getting free ringtones, wallpapers and a customized voicemail from a favorite player.

The campaign was a success and even outperformed TV, online and in-store activities.

59. Itching for An Audience.

Universal used banner and text mobile ads to generate excitement for its upcoming picture, The Wolfman. The campaign was atypical in that it included an Auto-Play interactive Video Ad Unit where a visitor could tap the link and be taken the movie's mobile website.

On The Wolfman mobile site, the consumer could view a video, read about the movie and even buy tickets.

The results were excellent as awareness increased 69%, and incredibly 31% of participants stated their intent to see the film. Unfortunately, the film got bad reviews, which surely hurt ticket sales. Rotten Tomatoes, a popular review site, gave the film 2 out of 5 stars. Ouch!

60. Recording Stars.

To engage the youth market and drive pre-orders of one of its artist's new singles, a major record label turned to mobile ads as its advertising method of choice. The company created a focused, mobile advertising campaign for the new single, and focused its efforts on raising the band's profile among its desired youth audience.

The record label targeted over 1 million iPod touch users (via its mobile provider's network) that segmented out by their focus on music, entertainment and gaming applications. Two separate ad formats were used to achieve the label's campaign objectives. Animated banners presented a great way to raise the profile of the up-and-coming band, and to promote its single, thus providing an added layer of brand messaging for the user.

To drive pre-orders of the single, the record label tapped its mobile provider's ad unit, which focused on driving users to iTunes to buy the song.

The results of the campaign were positive. The company's banners delivered click-through rates of 4.32% across the campaign period, thus indicating a clear impact on user engagement and awareness.

That's not all. There was a significant uplift in pre-orders of the single and over the course of the campaign click-through rates remained consistent at 0.85%. Perhaps even more impressive is the fact that the mobile ad campaign pushed that new single into the UK top 10 tracks on iTunes, and eventually helped it peak at number 3 on the Top 100 chart. Amazing!

61. Ahead of the Game.

VEGAS.com's mission is to be the most customer friendly, innovative and comprehensive Las Vegas travel company. As part of its strategic marketing plan, the company uses mobile ads to extend ad coverage for vacationers who are on the go. Through its mobile efforts, the online travel company has been able to reach new customers and drive measurable return on investment.

The company has been using AdWords to promote its site for years, and recently began targeting people who were researching Las Vegas travel opportunities on the go using their mobile devices. It launched a mobile website and began using mobile ads to raise awareness of its services.

Using a mix of text and image ads, the company linked potential customers to its mobile website, and/or to call a customer contact center.

Through its efforts, VEGAS.com achieved an almost 20% click-through rate (CTR) on some of its iPhone-targeted campaigns. Using click-to-call and click-to-website ads, the company was able to access a large and expanding audience of individuals who access the Internet from their mobile devices.

VEGAS.com has also started displaying ads on iPhone, Android and other mobile devices that use regular Internet browsers. The company considers itself to be "ahead of the game" in terms of mobile advertising, and it continues to tap into more mobile tools to expand its presence in the "on the go" reservation realm.

62. Driving the Masses.

Jaguar is just one of many automobile manufacturers that's testing the waters of mobile advertising. The luxury carmaker uses banner ads on mobile portals such as cars.mobi, MSN.mobi, Yahoo Mobile and the Admob ad network to generate traffic to its sites and increase its reach.

Targeting 35- to 54-year-old males, Jaguar looks for potential customers with high household income levels and the desire to drive a classy vehicle. Using its mobile site, the carmaker entices visitors to view videos, download wallpapers (featuring pictures of its cars, naturally) and interact in other ways via their mobile devices.

Jaguar received 30 million ad impressions across the mobile Internet, and 140,000 new visitors to the Jaguar XF mobile site, during the first six months of its mobile ad campaign. During the same period, 12,000 videos and 18,000 wallpapers were downloaded.

Users who got past Jaguar's home page dwelled on the site for an average of two minutes, the company reports, and 1.2% of those visitors requested an email brochure by entering email into the mobile site.

Another 2.6% of visitors located the nearest dealer to arrange a test drive, for a total of 3,640 test-drives. The automaker has since expanded its mobile campaign and relies on it to help "drive" traffic across its sites into the showroom.

63. Driving to the Dealer.

Land Rover successfully used mobile advertising to increase excitement around its Range RoverSports vehicle, and to entice prospects to visit their dealers.

Targeting affluent, adult males, the mobile advertising linked consumers to a landing page where the visitors could click to watch a video, click to call and/or find a retailer nearby.

(A landing page is a mobile web page that is designed as the location to further the process from ad to offer.

It can be separate from your mobile website or it can be one of the pages on your mobile website.)

The results were that 88% of the visitors clicked on the video, 3% clicked to the call, and 9% used the dealer locator. While this effort took place in 2008, it demonstrates that giving visitors a choice of how they want to contact you is always a good idea.

Location-Specific Advertising

64. Location, location…sound familiar?

Location is an important part in getting response from mobile ads.

In the U.S., an ad network wanted to test the importance of location to response rates. It signed up McDonald's to test responses. A mobile ad was sent to a consumer when he was near a McDonald's restaurant. The test would measure click through rates.

The results: click through rate at 2.49% or 13 times more than the average click through rate for an online, banner ad. And, of those people who clicked on the ad, 39% asked for more information on how to get to the restaurant.

The same test was repeated in Finland. The results were even stronger with a 7% click through rate.

Again, this indicates that importance of location in creating instant-awareness, interest and action. It is another reason why it is important to learn about location-based mobile social media.

Miscellaneous

65. Every Business Can....

By now you know that businesses strive for a high click through rate on their mobile ads. They figure that the more people who click on an ad, the more likely they will be sold when they get to their mobile site.

Here is an idea that does just the opposite. Consider running a mobile ad campaign designed to get awareness rather than clicks. The clicks cost you money. The impressions do not. The more impressions you get, the more awareness there is about your business.

The next time you test your mobile ads, don't just run the ad that performs the best on click through rates, but consider what if. What if you also run the ad that performed the worst? After all, if no one clicks on that worst "click through rate" ad, all the impressions from it are free.

And, who knows, maybe the increased awareness from all those "free" impressions will boost the response rate of your better performing ads.

Ready, Set, Go!

From this chapter you learned how mobile ads work and exactly how companies are using this mode of reaching customers, obtaining critical data about those individuals, building their opt-in databases and positioning themselves ahead of the pack in their respective industries.

Now it's your turn. Using the information you've learned in this chapter – and the social media, proximity marketing, QR code and mobile app advice and examples that you'll read about in upcoming chapters – you'll be ready to launch a mobile ad campaign that blends well with your existing advertising efforts.

In the resource section of this book you'll find a list of trusted providers that we carefully selected and included for your convenience. Check out these options as you prepare your own mobile ad campaign, and be sure to interview and research any partners that you chose to work with.

In the next chapter we'll look at some different types of mobile campaigns that fall under the "location-based mobile social media campaign" umbrella. Flip to the next page to get started…

Location Based Mobile Social Media/Foursquare

In real estate, location is everything. The concept is gaining ground quickly on the Internet, where location-based marketing has become a hot buzzword among companies looking to cash in on consumers' love of "letting everyone know" where they are and what they're up to.

The biggest player in the location-based market right now is Foursquare. Primarily for letting your friends know where you are and figuring out where they are, Foursquare allows users to collect points, prize "badges" and coupons for going about their everyday business. Users can link their Foursquare activities to their social networking accounts, such as Twitter and Facebook, thus increasing the service's reach.

Businesses are also using location-based services like Foursquare. Retailers, for example, can use location-based marketing to offer promotions to new customers, lure back past clients and reward their best customers (or the "Mayors," a title awarded to individuals by Foursquare). Using the service and a mobile phone, clients share their locations and chat up the great deals they've received from your business.

The concept is taking hold. New research from the Mobile Marketing Association has found location-based mobile marketing to yield significantly more response than other mobile ad formats. While 28% of mobile phone users noticed non-targeted ads on mobile websites, for example, and 37% noticed non-location-based ads while text messaging, almost 50% took action when presented with a location-based targeted ad.

The MMA says that about 10% of mobile consumers use a location-based service once a week, be it a map or business-location service. Younger consumers are more apt to embrace the medium, with 22% of those with ages between 25 and 34 using location-based services once or more each week.

Here are a few more quick facts about location-based marketing from the MMA:

- ✓ 63% of iPhone owners use location services at least once a week

- ✓ Respondents said they use location-based services most frequently to "locate nearby points of interest, shops or services"

- ✓ Consumers are interested in allowing their phone to automatically share their location in exchange for a reward, such as free mobile applications and mobile coupons.

As you can see, the opportunities abound in the location-based marketing field, where right now, it's only the most tech- and social networking-savvy companies that are diving into it. The good news is that this is a fairly inexpensive and easy way to reach out to existing and new customers via mobile marketing. It is something you should check out for your business.

In the next section we'll help you get your company in on the leading edge of this marketing method. We'll start by showing you different ways to jump in, and then round out the chapter with some examples of pioneering firms that are already reaping the rewards of this mobile marketing method.

How to Use Location-Based Mobile Social Media

There are myriad ways that companies can use location-based social media to grow their bottom lines. Here are a few strategies that you can put to work in your own business today:

✓ **Ask customers to check in and post reviews about your company.** Foursquare is a viral marketing method, meaning that your customers do the work for you by talking up the great experience, good deal or other positive event that took place at your location. The service allows users to see where their "friends" have been within three hours of a specific update, whether they were eating, enjoying a movie or staying at a hotel. Ask customers to "check in" and post positive comments about their experiences and you'll be surprised at how quickly the good word will spread. Offer a discount or special deal for those users who proffer up favorable reviews and your stable of marketing mavens will grow exponentially.

✓ **Make them mayors.** A user who checks in the most at a restaurant, store, gym or other location becomes the "mayor" of that location. Then, other users try to knock that person out of that position by becoming the mayor themselves. A quick look at the Foursquare users on your Twitter account, for example, shows just how ferocious the fight for that coveted title can get. You can leverage the situation by offering special treatment to your "mayor." Put the person's name on a plaque on the front counter, give he or she discounts or name a new menu item after that person to encourage location-based service users to physically visit your location often.

✓ **Give them something to do.** Everyone likes to feel like they are part of something, and that their role is important. You can use Foursquare to create a to-do list for your mobile phone users. Come up with a contest that targets individuals who visit your shop in person, and offer perks (like the ones listed above for mayors) that entice consumers to complete their to-do lists. A bakery, for example, might use the to-do list to get customers thinking about the next cupcake flavor that should be added to the shop's lineup.

The opportunities to exploit location-based marketing for your own marketing purposes are limited only by your own imagination, so be creative with these campaigns. Like most of the mobile marketing world, there's really no right or wrong, as long as you respect your users' privacy and right to opt out of such campaigns at any time.

According to Foursquare, millions of users turn to its service every day to help them find their friends and explore their world. Whether they are checking out a new restaurant or visiting their favorite store, they are sharing their activities and loyalty with their social network, earning badges and points along the way. For brands, for example, Foursquare offers a unique way to stay engaged with followers no matter where they are in the world.

At the heart of this mobile marketing strategy is "Foursquare Page," or your custom homepage on

Foursquare, the epicenter of all brand engagement. Your fans can "follow" your Page (similar to the one on Twitter), allowing them to see tips you've left around the world. Your page can be customized to include your brand imagery, links to other websites and can be located at a custom URL for your brand.

Sounds enticing, doesn't it? Well, let's look at how some companies are already using location-based services mobile social media to expand their horizons and grow their profits.

Restaurant and Retail

66. Not Your Average Burger Joint.

There is a small chain of specialty burger restaurants in the Midwest that's tapping into social networking check-in application Foursquare for mobile marketing. In fact, within just a few months of rolling out its campaign, the company already had nearly 1,500 customers check in over 6,000 times on the restaurant's Foursquare profile page.

To get there, the company started by educating staff members about the location-based service and the special promotions that it planned to offer through the marketing medium. The goal was to spread the word to customers, in hopes that those Foursquare users would turn around and disseminate the information even deeper into their banks of "friends."

Take the free burger that the "mayor" gets when crowned. The award is given to the person whom Foursquare identifies as having visited and "checked in" the most via mobile phone at one of the restaurant's locations. The burger is a popular prize that Foursquare users vie for, although the chain also offers smaller prizes to those individuals who add "tips" to the company's profile page.

To reward those who don't achieve mayoral status, the restaurant identifies the next highest- ranking members and enters them into a "Loyalty Club," where members gain access to a menu designed specifically for them. The chain's management is bullish on location-based mobile social media's potential, and plans to continue using the strategy as part of its overall marketing mix.

67. Pizza-Centric Social Networking.

Companies are also using mobile marketing in conjunction with social networking. The two go hand-in-hand, particularly because those individuals who tend to be most active on sites like Twitter and Facebook are also avid cell phone users. Touting iPhones, Droids and Blackberrys, these folks are a natural target for companies looking to beef up their customer pipelines and databases.

Papa John's is one company that recognizes the value of social networking. The pizza franchise uses Facebook on several fronts, including an engaging ad that drove people to become a fan of its Facebook Page.

Fans were notified on three different dates via an Update from the Papa John's Page, and were then directed to the company's website to receive their promotional code for the pizza.

The campaign was a raging success. According to Papa John's, the company added 125,000 fans within a day, and has since grown that number to over 200,000 today.

Papa John's has also used social networking (Facebook "Gifts") to give away virtual pizzas. In fact, it has given way a couple hundred thousand of those pizzas. Using this strategy, people can send their friends a "gift" in the form of a Papa John's ad for pizza.

The company reports that ROI on both promotions exceeded expectations. For example, the number of fans that it added more than doubled expectations. More Papa John's campaigns are in the works, and will likely include some type of social networking strategy that maximizes the company's marketing investment with little additional money or effort.

Sports and Entertainment

68. Bravo TV asks Viewers to Join Andy on Foursquare.

Cable network Bravo TV has amassed a cult-like following for its innovative reality shows. From the

"Housewives of…" series to Patty Stanger's Millionaire Matchmaker Show to its outrageous real estate listing programs, the network is especially popular with the hip, mobile phone-toting crowd.

This past New Year's Eve, Bravo brought one of its most visible personalities into the world of location-based marketing. Andy Cohen is Bravo's Senior Vice President of Original Programming and Development, and is responsible for overseeing the network's current development and production slate of over 24 different shows.

Using the title "Watch What Happens Live: Andy's New Year's Eve Party" Bravo mobilized its location-based campaign by encouraging users to follow Bravo TV on Foursquare and check in on New Year's Eve. In return, users were entered for the chance to have their names and faces appear on screen during the show.

Participation in the event was only available to those who follow Bravo on Foursquare. For those who didn't want to participate in the Bravo NYE special, the network offered the option to either check in [off the grid] during the special or un-follow Bravo during the special. "Don't worry, you won't lose any of your Bravo badges!" the network told its anxious viewers.

The campaign attracted a high number of viewers who really did want to see what Andy was up to on the biggest night of the year, and who wanted the chance to have their faces and addresses displayed on their television screens. There's little doubt the Bravo will use similar promotions in the future as it looks to increase its stable of viewers who are hungry for innovative, cutting-edge television content.

Miscellaneous

69. Paper and Packaging

You don't have to own a trendy restaurant or cool gift shop to take advantage of location- based marketing. An international parcel service proved that in 2010 when it launched a mobile marketing campaign that included location- and context-sensitive messages aimed at prospective customers.

The parcel service rolled out the campaign in major cities where users were made aware of the company's locations when they accessed specific websites via their cell phones. (This "ad-inject" process is much like what you see on sites like Pandora, where simply logging onto the service pulls up a few "local" ads for firms that are located in your area.)

With more that 75% of its parcel deliveries being ordered online, this company was a particularly good candidate for the location-based social media, which allowed it to interact with customers through mobile methods. Expect to see more companies taking advantage of this "localized" marketing approach that leverages not only mobile, but that also whets users' appetites for convenient, locally-based products and services.

Ready, Set, Go!

Social media-location based campaigns have universal appeal that can be used at pretty much any type of company that services a base of loyal customers, whether they have physical locations or not. In fact, there are the two main categories of Foursquare users, according to the company:

Brands with physical locations, like Starbucks, Sports Authority or the Museum of Modern Art. The Foursquare Merchant Platform offers easy tools for engaging customers.

Brands that are not tied to a specific physical location, like a consumer packaged good, TV channel, university, manufacturer, or an upcoming movie release.

Foursquare has worked with hundreds of brand partners to reach millions of users on Foursquare, including Bravo TV, Louis Vuitton, The New York Times, Havaianas, Microsoft Windows Live, the History Channel, Syracuse University, Red Bull and NASA. For these types of partners, Foursquare provides two main marketing tools – Pages and Custom Badges - that help lead consumers and fans to do interesting things in their neighborhoods and communities.

As you learned in this chapter, location-based mobile social media can be a highly effective way to attract new customers, reward your most loyal clients and tap into a viral advertising format that many companies have yet to discover. As mobile and location-based applications continue to grow in popularity, you'll want to integrate them into your overall marketing mix and use them to your advantage.

Now it's time to turn our sights to proximity marketing, yet another innovative mobile technique that can help leverage marketing dollars and closely target desirable customer segments. Flip to the next chapter to get started.

Proximity Marketing

If you've ever been standing in your driveway keying a phrase into your mobile web browser, only to be hit with an ad for your local plumber, then you've been a target of proximity marketing. As one of the more untapped aspects of mobile marketing, this "bluecasting" or "Bluetooth marketing," is particularly effective for companies looking to target current and prospective customers that are located in precise geographical locations.

In fact, to say proximity marketing is precise would be an understatement. That's because it targets the spot where the recipient is standing, and not his or her country, state or city. The secret to the method's success lies in the transmitters that marketing services place in select public locations. The devices emit signals to mobile phones and computers whose Bluetooth feature is enabled within 100 yards or so of the actual devices.

The marketing messages are sent to the user's phone, which receives an alert letting the recipient know that free content is available for download. Once the user grants permission, the content can be delivered to the phone.

What makes Bluetooth marketing so attractive is the fact that its reach and downloads are both highly measurable. Using this mobile marketing method, you can see exactly whom your ads are reaching and which individuals are taking the next step by downloading the free content.

Proximity marketing also includes the local ads that pop up on the bottom of a mobile phone's screen when, for example, a user keys in a location to Google Maps. In an almost magical fashion, companies are able to reach out to users who are, say, trying to find the nearest gas station. While they're at it, why not stop at the local Subway and grab a few subs for $1 off? These types of proximity marketing campaigns are gaining ground in an "on the go" world that's becoming more and more reliant on its cell phones.

Despite the fact that proximity marketing is a nascent activity, there are already many good examples of how companies are using it to expand business, attract new customers and grow their databases. The Mobile Marketing Association, for example, recently published a series of case studies for successful proximity and mobile marketing campaigns.

The MMA case studies highlight what was done right, and they describe the marketing concept and the approach taken, and also report on the results as number of downloads/participation rates. For example, the group says coupons are one technique that carries over well to the proximity marketing space.

Specifically, this technique involves making special offers available that can be redeemed simply by showing the phone at the register. There's nothing to print, nothing to mail and nothing for the consumer to carry around and accidentally "forget" at home. The coupon is right there on a mobile device, ready to redeem.

Now it's time to get an inside look at exactly how companies are using proximity marketing to reach out to customers, expand their brand recognition and build their businesses. In the next section you'll see exactly how these innovative campaigns work and what kind of ROI they're delivering to companies of all sizes.

70. Making Movies.

Intent on reaching the 15- to 19-year-old male demographic and drawing it into movie theatres while also building overall market share, a major motion picture production company developed a Bluetooth proximity campaign for one its movies.

The movie, which appealed to that young, male audience, was promoted for four weeks leading up to its national release. Visitors to cinemas who had Bluetooth enabled on their phones received a free message to their devices asking if they would like to view the movie trailer as a download. According to the company, the goal was to reach the target demographic while they were "in the mood" for a movie.

Anyone who accepted the invitation was able to view the trailer immediately, via his or her mobile phones. Until the trailer was manually deleted, it remained on the devices. Recipients were also prompted to download calendar reminders that were set for the movie's release date.

The campaign was conducted in what scientists would call a "controlled" environment in that the movie was not promoted via any other means at the movie theatres, nor was it publicized using traditional media.

Within 30 days the movie trailer received over 150,000 unique downloads, indicating a high interest among the target demographic for the movie. The download numbers exceeded the movie production company's expectations, and prompted it to consider proximity marketing for future releases.

Restaurants and Retail

71. Time to Make the Doughnuts.

Krispy Kreme's first advertising campaign in the U.K. market included billboard calls-to-action used to drive brand awareness and customer loyalty via Bluetooth downloads.

The doughnut company placed electronic billboards across a number of railway stations, which prompt consumers to "turn on Bluetooth now and receive your FREE voucher."

The offer allowed participants to redeem a generous 12 free doughnuts as part of the Festive Double Dozen Deal simply by showing the mobile voucher in Krispy Kreme stores.

The campaign, which was supported by print advertising, was a huge success for the company in a brand new market that was unfamiliar with Krispy Kreme's "melt in your mouth" pastries. During the 15-day campaign, Krispy Kreme generated over 48,000 total downloads.

72. Helping Them Smell Good,

Lynx (or Axe in the U.S.) is a brand of male grooming products, owned by the British/Dutch company Unilever and marketed towards young males. To promote its new pocket-sized spray on university campuses, the company launched a proximity marketing campaign aimed at young college students.

The campaign ran in university student unions across the UK, where Lynx installed highly visible floor vinyls in the "download zones" to increase awareness of the campaign.

Users were encouraged to download a simple branded dating application. The company reported positive results for the campaign, which averaged over 500 downloads per day, per university.

Sports & Entertainment

73. Weekend of Proximity

When music fans gather in one place, something magical happens, particularly if you throw proximity marketing into the mix. A radio station found this out recently when it employed the marketing tactic at one of its free, live music events.

This isn't the radio station's first foray into the world of Web 2.0 marketing. In fact, its most popular, annual event is recognized as the world's largest-ever virtual world music festival, and the first in-world broadcast by a major media corporation.

At a recent event, the station installed and managed a number of systems covering the massive areas in and around the main and secondary staging. Large posters were posted in and around these areas, and encouraged attendees to "switch on their Bluetooth" to receive free content.

Some of that content included mobile phone wallpapers of the bands leaving the stage immediately following the performances. Needless to say, these downloads were in big demand on concert day.

Over the duration of the weekend, more than 2,000 attendees received free mobile phone content to their phone. The numbers represent about 7% of the total audience. Not a bad turnout considering the company had no idea exactly how many users had a Bluetooth-enabled phone with them at the concert.

74. Rolling Them Out.

A leading mobile phone retailer based in India used proximity marketing recently to increase the number of walk-ins to its retail outlets during their annual sale. The company's goal was to communicate a series of promotional offers to a select group of customers, at a time when they were ready to receive relevant content.

The company segmented customers based on their phones as lower end, mid-segment and high-end handsets, and then delivered relevant communication to those targets by delivering offers that matched their mobile profile. Mid-segment customers, for example, received offers to upgrade their memory cards at a discounted price.

Bluetooth networking devices placed in shopping malls, restaurants and other places where young people hang out were used to deliver the messages to those phones. The mall-based devices, for example, delivered promotional messages that prompted customers to explore their nearest mobile phone retail outlet, and provided an address for that location.

According to the company, over 50,000 users responded to the proximity marketing campaign via 20 Bluetooth device locations. The actual number of users who made their way to retail locations as a result of the campaign totaled more than 4,000, with individual retail locations reporting 45% increases in foot traffic during the campaign periods.

Trade shows

75. A Beautiful Bluetooth.

Using proximity marketing at a trade show can help lure more prospects to your booth. Duri Cosmetics used Bluetooth marketing to attract prospects that attended a major trade show for beauty salon and spa products.

The company sent a message to Bluetooth-enabled phones, and if the message was accepted, the prospect was encouraged to visit Duri Cosmetic's mobile website, download a video of Duri products, and/or visit the company's booth. The mobile site was also promoted on signage and other promotional materials at the booth.

At the show, 26% of the visitors had Bluetooth-enabled phones and about 13% of them downloaded the Duri Cosmetics content. While there was no precise numbers of how many more prospects visited the booth, Duri Cosmetic executives stated that the show was a success.

Ready, Set, Go!

Proximity marketing is probably the least used of all of the mobile marketing campaign strategies, but that doesn't mean you can afford to overlook it. In fact, this method produces significant results (as you will read in this chapter) in exchange for a small money and time investment.

By setting up "hotspots" in areas where you know your target customer will frequent, you can all but assure your chances of reaching them through their mobile phones via proximity marketing.

Just ask the plumbers and real estate agents who continually pops up on my Tweetcaster app every time I use it. The opportunities are pretty much limitless and the terrain largely untapped. Now is the time to get started with a simple proximity marketing campaign that will allow you to test the waters and adjust as needed.

In the next section you'll learn about QR codes and how to use these 2D barcodes as part of your next mobile marketing campaign.

QR Codes

The QR code appeared first in Japan in 1994. A QR (quick response) code is essentially a barcode with spots instead of the traditional bars. A QR code is also referred to as a 2D barcode since it is a two dimensional code. These codes contain data that can be scanned or read by a smartphone.

The reason QR codes are so valuable to a business is that the code can instantly take a customer to your website or to any information. For example, if your QR code contains data that is your URL, the customer can be taken to your web page on his phone.

Once you make the physical world, clickable, almost anything is possible. Today, QR codes are used for mobile coupons, gift cards, business cards, event promotions, email campaigns, downloading apps and more. If you post a QR code on your door, a customer who arrives after you close can check out what you provide by taking a photo of your QR code, have the phone read it, and get more information at your website.

A QR code is a novel concept in the US. There is no cost to create a QR code if you use one of the free generators online (see section at the end of the book). If you use a QR code in your business, you will be noticed.

Frankly, I have a QR reader on my iPhone and it works great. If you have an iPhone, I recommend downloading Qrafter. Yes, it's free!

Libraries

76. The Paperless Chase.

If you don't think QR codes are right for your business, think again. If libraries are using codes effectively, so should you.

Libraries have embraced the use of coding for a wide range of informational reasons.

For example, Lawrence University Seeley G. Mudd Library uses QR codes to direct visitors to their virtual tour, electronic music resources, mobile website, and to begin text messages to the interlibrary loan office. QR codes are so useful at this library that they even provide a QR code informational guide to help visitors understand them.

Boise State University's Albertsons Library has a mobile website and a Twitter page. It uses QR codes to take people to these sites. They even provide tips on creating effective codes, and which readers to use, based on the specific mobile phone.

Charities

77. Clean up.

To get the public's support for the restoration of the Gulf, the Women of the Storm started a celebrity supported "Be the One" campaign. The objective of this effort was to get signatures for their petition to restore the Gulf.

A QR code was generated that took users to a mobile website where they could watch the video and sign the petition. Another code was created to be used on t-shirts and online. Overall, the petition received more than 117.000 signatures.

Media

78. Hot Off-the-Press.

Sometimes beauty is in the palm of the beholder. At least that's what Sports Illustrated made happen with QR codes in their 2010 Swimsuit Issue.

Here, all you needed to do was to browse that issue, and use your camera phone to snap some photos of the "beautiful" QR codes. In moments, your phone would display the behind the scenes video of these models' photo shoots.

79. Out of the Closet.

The online fashion retailer Bluefly used QR codes on their TV commercials to increase the size of their audience. It was the first time a national retailer used bar codes in their television advertising.

The TV advertising showed short clips of their celebrities' "Closet Confessions" interviews. On the TV screen, a QR code appeared. Once it was scanned, a viewer would be taken to a short segment of the show, and then be offered a discount on purchases at bluefly.com.

80. Lost and Found.

In the last episode of "Lost," HBO used a QR code to promote their series "True Blood." The 2D bar code was made to be consistent with the show's branding; code's design was black and red with a touch of blood. It ran at the end of the 30-second commercial.

Retail

81. It's in the Jeans.

Gap added QR codes to in-store posters that linked consumers to product reviews and styling ideas for a new line of pants. Gap used a mobile site to provide the information.

In addition, Gap added a QR code to the direct mail campaign that connected to a video interview with a Gap designer and a coupon.

Events

82. All that Jazz.

QR codes are also a way to be environmentally friendly. At the Rochester Jazz Festival, a QR code was used on posters to deliver the information usually found in the printed brochures. The QR code linked to a mobile website where the day's event and activities were outlined. The organizers even got sponsors to pay for the coded posters by adding their logos to it.

Who knew QR codes could be a way to save trees?

Real Estate

83. Home Alone.

Real estate agents can't be everywhere at once when it comes to selling a home. Buyers often drive by a home and judge the home by its appearance.

A few agents are adding QR codes to their "For Sale" signage. A prospective buyer can take a photo of the code and be taken to a mobile website with all the details about the house, along with photos and/or videos. How great would it be to instantly know if a home is the right size and the right price range?

Of course, a sign with QR code will stands out from all other "For Sale" signs.

Meetings

84. Business Cards.

It is common to exchange business cards at meetings, trade shows and even social events. More businesses are adding a QR code on their business cards that link to their company's website.

The QR code can also be used to help save a person's contact information.

Restaurants

85. Tasty Codes.

One restaurant decided to use QR codes to increase sales of meals that were not selling and as a way to introduce new dishes.

When a customer opened a menu, there were QR codes next to the food items. By scanning a QR code, the diner would be linked to a video where the chef demonstrated what went into the dish, how long it cooked, and, of course, the actual revealing of the tasty-looking meal.

Miscellaneous

86. Every Business can...

Use QR codes creatively in your business. They will help you to stand out from the competition and at the same time inform your customers.

Put a QR code on your storefront, on your business card, and on any printed message with your business name. Put a QR code on your ads and even your website. Some designers have used these codes on clothing and purses. Why not have your company T-shirt or to support your local softball team?

Ready, Set, Go!

As you learned firsthand in this chapter, QR codes play a key role in many mobile marketing campaigns. These two-dimensional codes can easily be scanned by smartphone cameras, which then pull up text, photos, videos, music and URLs that you can use to promote your business.

In fact, QR codes have become one of the most "mobile-friendly" ways to point customers to online resources, even when they're out and about. In the next chapter we'll introduce you to mobile apps and show you how to use them in your own business.

Mobile Apps

The mobile application business is booming. It is estimated that revenue from mobile apps will reach $15 billion in 2011 with the number of mobile app downloads to reach 17.7 billion.

Mobile applications allow consumers to download via the mobile Internet specially developed content from a business. Apps can work on one type of phone or across multiple platforms.

According to Nielsen (June 2010) the top mobile apps in the US are Facebook, Google Maps and the Weather Channel. The most popular categories are games; news; maps; social networking and music.

Any product or service that is currently provided, and almost any idea can be turned into a mobile application. There are companies that have used mobile apps to provide instant updates to customers, attract new customers, and generate added value. The key is to decide if your mobile app is going to provide a positive return on investment.

There are so many apps, you may hear someone say "there's an app for that." That may be very true. Here are some of things mobile apps let you do from your mobile device.

- ✓ Securely encrypt and store financial and personal data
- ✓ Watch TV from your phone
- ✓ Turn the phone into a virtual keyboard
- ✓ Scan documents into the phone with the built-in camera
- ✓ Track your diet and fitness plan
- ✓ Track your business expenses
- ✓ Locate the nearest bank, gas station, drug store, etc.
- ✓ Host web conferences from your phone
- ✓ Print from your phone
- ✓ Create job estimates and invoices

Some predict that the demand for apps will decline in 2013 as consumers move to mobile websites and the leading apps are preloaded in mobile phones. Right now, that prediction looks debatable as more and more businesses develop more and more apps.

87. Here an App, There an App, Everywhere an App App.

To start the process of generating ideas for your own mobile application, here is a list of the 20 categories in the Mac App Store for an iPad, along with the best selling product.

- Book: Thomas and Friends
- Business: PrintCentral
- Education: Star Walk
- Entertainment: Ions
- Finance: Money
- Games: Angry Birds
- Healthcare and Fitness: Calorie Tracker
- Lifestyle: CraigsPro
- Medical: Muscle Trigger Points
- Music: TuneIn Radio
- Navigation: MotionX GPS
- News: New York Post
- Photography: Camera for iPad
- Productivity: Penultimate
- Reference: World Atlas
- Social Networking: Facebook
- Sports: Football Bowl Squares
- Travel: FlightBoard

- Utilities: Skyfire Web Browser
- Weather: Weather HD

88. An App to Add Value.

One way a business can meet the needs of its consumers is to provide a mobile app.

Constant Contact is a leader in providing small businesses with software and services for managing email campaigns. Since many small business owners and managers wanted to keep track of their email campaigns while away from the office, they created an application for the iPhone and iPod Touch.

The free application Quickview provided the most important information to its customers. The result of this effort: Quickview has been downloaded thousands of times, and at one point, was the 23rd most popular application in the free business category.

89. An App to Create Buzz.

NetSuite is the industry's first and only Software-as-a-Service (SaaS) business software that supports an entire company—from accounting/enterprise resource planning (ERP) to customer relationship management (CRM) and web capabilities—in a single, integrated and powerful business management software solution.

Just because there were few apps in the B2B field, it did not stop them from coming up with the first cloud computing Enterprise Resource app for the iPhone and iPod Touch.

Not only did the app get buzz for being the first mobile application in this area, but it also had 5,000 downloads in the first month. Their app has also shown to prospects that the company is aggressive and willing to do what is necessary to standout and innovate.

90. Download Me.

There are hundreds of thousands of mobile apps on the market. It is a gold rush for those who create a winning mobile app for Android or the iPhone. It is fools gold for those who believe their app can breakthrough the clutter without marketing support.

OpenTable is a successful online service that lets you make dinner reservations. To attract new users, OpenTable developed a mobile app so a consumer on the move could easily reserve a table from their mobile device.

The OpenTable Android app was promoted using cost per click text mobile ads. To get a better return on its ad dollar, OpenTable tested different ad messages and expanded its spending to improve its return on investment.

The results were that the daily downloads more than doubled during the test, with downloads being initiated by more then 75 different types of Android devices.

91. Paint it Green

ColorSnap is an app from Sherwin-Williams that let users take photos of their surroundings and match those colors to the paint colors from the company. In addition, you could use the app to locate a nearby Sherwin-Williams retailer.

A two-day mobile ad campaign ran across 3,000 iPhone sites. The results were that daily downloads increased by 500%. Before the campaign, the ColorSnap app was poorly ranked in the utility category of the app store. After the campaign, the app went to #18.

Even after the campaign was over, the app continued to be highly ranked leading to even more downloads.

Ready, Set, Go!
Mobile apps are all the rage right now, with consumers and businesses downloading a wide variety of both "free" and "paid" applications to their smartphones and computers. If you have an idea for an app, research it, find out what it will cost you, and

if you move ahead, be prepared to support it with a marketing campaign. It's a jungle out there.

92: More Mobile Marketing Ideas

I have added many more mobile marketing ideas in this section. Review all of these ideas, as you never know where you will discover something that you may want to try for your business.

Auto dealers

- It is difficult to sell a car when your dealership is closed. However, place a QR code on the windshields of cars or the windows of your dealership, so prospects can get information needed via text, pictures, and videos on a mobile site.

Beauty Salons

- Send a text to customers to confirm their appointment a few days ahead of time. The customer needs to reply with a Y or N. You want to keep your salon full and not lose revenue.

Bookstores

- Use your mobile database to find out the interest of your visitors. In that way, you can text new book arrivals that are most likely to turn into a sale. For example, if Bob signs up to your loyalty program and states an interest in books about sports, send a text about the new arrival of sports books.

Cleaners

- Send a customer a text when his/her clothes arrive.
- When a customer forgets to pick up his/her clothes for two or more days, send a text alert.
- Provide an incentive to new people who move into the area with a special discount on the anniversary of their arrival. Every year, text messages a special coupon on this date.

Electronic stores

- Buy mobile ads that lead prospects to your landing page or mobile website. You can pinpoint your target customer and tailor your advertising message so it's more effective.

Health Clubs

- Let your members know when their membership is about to expire, with a special discount offer via a text message.
- Buy mobile ads based on zip code at the end of the year--the time when people resolve to work out after the New Year.
- Announce new classes to your members via text message.

Hospitality: Hotels, Motels

- Text rate discounts, special holiday promotions
- Text reservation confirmation and free upgrade
- Announce a new location
- Create VIP memberships
- Get feedback using surveys
- Special holiday promotions

Medical Offices-Doctors, Dentists, Chiropractors

- Text message your patients a day or two before an appointment, to confirm. They text reply Y for Yes or N for N. Don't lose revenue when a patient forgets to cancel.

- Text message a reminder to patients when it's time to set up an appointment, such as it has been six months since their last appointment.
- Other SMS ideas: Payment reminders, birthday messages, special screenings, testing day alerts or schedule changes initiated by the doctor.

Movie Theater
- Build a mobile database that includes your customer's interest based on genre. If a customer has an interest in comedy, you can send a text that announces when a new comedy arrives in your theater.
- When you know the attendance to a movie will be poor, text customers who have shown interest in that genre. Your movie may be a better alternative than another night in front of the TV.

Night Club
- Text message your customers who the entertainers will be that weekend.
- Have a text to win a contest to get free tickets to a show.

Pharmacy/Drug store

- Place a QR code on the door of your pharmacy. If someone drives by they will know when you are open. How often do you drive by a store that is closed but you can't read the hours it's open from your car?

- Text an alert to consumers reminding them that it's time to re-order their prescriptions.

- Allow a customer to order a prescription refill through their mobile phone after you send a text message.

Realtors

- You can't be everywhere at the same time, and you can't have an open house every weekend. There are many buyers who drive around an area searching for homes. They see a sign and may write down a number. Instead, consider posting a QR code on the sign that links to a visual presentation and details on the home.

- Develop a mobile database of those prospects looking to buy or rent based on their criteria. When a home, apartment or office space becomes available, be the first to alert these prospects using a text alert.

Restaurants:

- Even out slow periods such as between lunch and dinner. Offer a mobile coupon to show up at your restaurant during those hours. Double the discount if your customer brings a friend.
- Add a QR code to your menu. The QR code takes your guest to a short video showing how the food gets made, what it looks and tastes like. It's similar to having a short ad for new food items, slow food items, or your entire menu.
- Provide a Foursquare offer when a customer is in the neighborhood. For example, when your customer is at happy hour in a nearby bar, offer a free dessert to come to your restaurant.
- Send a text message to women about your happy hour where ladies get to drink at half off. And, don't' forget to remind the men on your mobile list as well.

- Send a text message to customers who are celebrating a birthday. If they show the text message at the door, they get a free meal.
- Other SMS ideas: Meal specials, new menu items, happy hour specials, new location alerts/grand openings, table availability
- Internal use--employee meetings, schedule changes

Retail stores--such as Clothing

- Text message a special sale to your loyal customers before the public is invited.
- New fashion arrivals.
- Add a QR code to your existing print ad.
- Other SMS ideas: New item announcements, contests or show this text for a discount

TV/Radio stations

- When your audience signs up with their mobile phone number, you can engage them in so many ways. It adds value to your station and can bring you even closer to your audience.
- Text message your customers about participating in a poll. You may find out what

they really want to listen to that day. And, whom they want on as a guest. You may get a better rating if you give your audience what they want.

- Contests using text messages are a way to get more viewers and/or listeners.
- If your database captured a member's favorite program, consider texting a reminder before your program starts.
- Text message your audience on weather alerts or school closings.

Visiting homes (cleaning carpets, exterminators, home repair, plumbers, etc.)

When you visit a customer's home, you have an opportunity to sign him up to your mobile database. This is important since your service is probably not one that is top of mind.

- Exterminator-text about seasonal check-ups based on termites, mice, etc.
- Carpet cleaners-text about the need for a carpet cleaning since its been 12 months since your visit.

- Home repair--text about things that need cleaned or checked due to the seasons.
- Plumbers-when something goes wrong with the plumbing, you want your customer to call you first. Place a sticker a QR code inside of a toilet tank that leads them to your website or your phone number.

Ready, Set, Go!

Don't be afraid to get out there and test the mobile marketing waters. You really don't have anything to lose, particularly since many of the methods being used are largely untested and welcomed by mobile phone users who haven't been jaded by a plethora of ads yet. Take your time, pick a strategy and go with it. You'll be surprised at the positive results!

Getting Even More From Going Mobile

93. A Gift From Google.

There are over 500 million local searches on Google each month. A local search is where a person adds a town or city name to the keyword. For example, instead of typing in "Italian Restaurant," the person types in "Italian Restaurants in Brooklyn." These local searches are now one out of every three searches on Google.

Due to this demand to find a local business, Google has changed the way its local search results appear. Instead of listing national companies first, Google features local businesses on Page One. Google knows that these local results are more relevant and meaningful to the person searching for a local business than a national company.

Google created 50 million local business listings. One of these listings has your business name on it. It is a free gift from Google that allows you take advantage of local search.

All your business has to do is claim it. It is free. You do not need to have a website to participate. But, you do need to have a physical address.

Best of all, if you use this listing wisely, it can improve your search results.

So far, only about 3% of the 50 million local businesses have claimed their Google Page. If you want to take advantage of this opportunity, you can find your page at places.google.com/business.

Having a Google Page is yet another way your business can be found on the mobile net.

94. Getting the Most from Your Google Listing.

After you claim your Google listing, it is time to get the most out of it. The more you develop your listing, the higher you will rank. Here is a list of items to include on your page:

- A description of your business
- Hours you are open
- If you take credit cards, and if so, which ones
- What categories to be listed in

- Videos
- Photos
- Reviews from customers

You should take the time to put a review system into your business. It is not that difficult to accomplish. Simply have index cards available at your business, and when a customer says something positive about your business, ask him if he wouldn't mind writing it down. Next, hire a service that inputs your reviews for you each month. The more positive reviews the higher you will appear in the rankings.

In fact, the next time you are doing a Google search on a local business, check the Google Places listings. In general, businesses that have more positive reviews rank higher.

95. Mobile Search-Step 1.

Mobile search is another opportunity for you to market your business. It is a marketing tool that can drive more visitors to your mobile website. You are planning to get a mobile friendly website, right?

Google suggests that having a website, a mobile website and a Google business listing is the best way to get the most out of your presence online.

In addition, to optimize your mobile site for local searches, it is best to have your business address on both your home page and your contact page. Your contact page should also include a map and directions.

When you register a mobile site name, Google prefers that you have a .mobi address. So, if your website is www.yourcompany.com, your mobile website should be www.yourcompany.mobi.

96. Mobile Search-Step 2.

You also need to be aware that mobile search is different than Internet search. When you started your business, you probably listed it on a number of search directories. At the very least, you submitted your site to the Google and Yahoo directories.

When it comes to mobile, you must submit your listing to the growing number of directories, mobile phone carrier directories, and even to auto-navigation services.

There are a number of online submission services that can handle this work for you. It won't cost you a lot of money, but it will give a consistent online and mobile presence for your business.

97. Mobile Search-Step 3.

When you have both a desktop and mobile version of your website, it is smart to redirect those who are visiting your desktop from a mobile device to your mobile website. This can be done automatically with an HTML code.

However, some website developers are trying to trick search engines to get higher rankings for their mobile site. They are using this feature in the wrong manner.

Let me explain what you must follow, so your mobile site is optimized for Google searches.

You must redirect your visitors from your website to your mobile website where the content is similar. For example, if a visitor types in www.yourcompany-homepage.com, you should automatically direct that visitor to your mobile site's home page. Do not direct that visitor to a page on your mobile site that has content totally different than your website's page. The Google algorithm will not reward your efforts, since it believes you are creating a negative user experience.

98. Mobile Apps.

Mobile apps are incredibly popular. Everyone seems to think they have an idea for an app that will make them wealthy. Usually, the idea is for another game app. After all, maybe your app will be the next Angry Birds. (If you are not aware, Angry Birds is the best selling game app. It has been downloaded millions of times at $4.99 each.)

The good news is that it is not that expensive to build an app. The bad news is that few apps become big winners.

If you have an idea for an app, my suggestion is to look for a mobile app developer at sites like elance.com, freelancer.com, and odesk.com. These online sites are a global marketplace for businesses that want to hire freelancers for less. You post your job on the site and people all over the world bid on it. As a rule, read the reviews and don't hire the cheapest bidder.

99. Mobile Website Strategy.

It is important to think about strategy in developing your mobile website. A mobile website is not a slimmer version of your desktop computer website. A mobile website is a complement to your site.

Your mobile website strategy needs to start by thinking about your customer. A customer is going to visit you from the mobile web because he is on the move. That means he is looking for content that he needs right away, or if he has some time, he is browsing for relevant information.

You mobile website can address a customer in both situations. A customer that has little time tends to want actionable content like the hours your open, where you are located, directions to your business, and a phone number to contact you.

A customer who is browsing your mobile site wants a positive experience as well. He wants to explore your site, but he is on a mobile device where navigation is easy and information is found fast.

Your mobile website strategy can and should address both situations.

100. Putting it All Together

Let me compare for you how the process compares-- online versus the mobile web--in the next two simple diagrams.

Process to get sales online with your current website

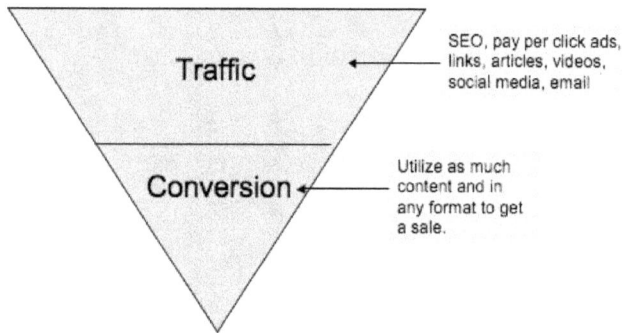

Traffic — SEO, pay per click ads, links, articles, videos, social media, email

Conversion — Utilize as much content and in any format to get a sale.

Your website should be phat and happy.

Process to get sales with a mobile website

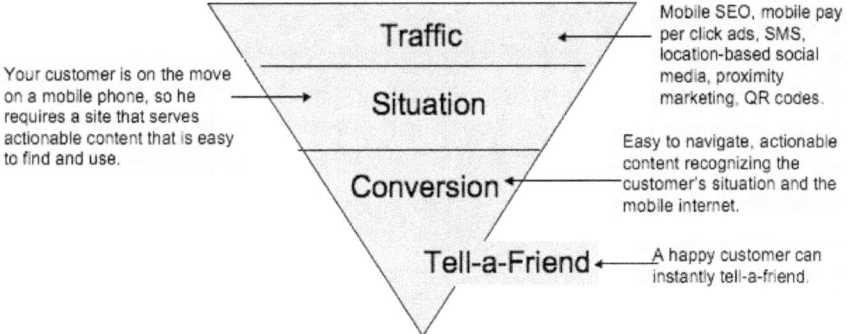

Traffic — Mobile SEO, mobile pay per click ads, SMS, location-based social media, proximity marketing, QR codes.

Your customer is on the move on a mobile phone, so he requires a site that serves actionable content that is easy to find and use. → Situation

Conversion — Easy to navigate, actionable content recognizing the customer's situation and the mobile internet.

Tell-a-Friend — A happy customer can instantly tell-a-friend.

Your mobile website should be fast, easy and actionable.

101. A Self-Serving Plug....

After reading this book, you may decide there are mobile marketing areas you want to explore.

As the CEO of A Smart Friend LLC & FirstMobileWebsite.com, I want to help you achieve your business goals using mobile marketing. We provide the following services to small businesses:

- Building the best mobile websites
- Setting up your Google places page
- Enhanced business listings & submission
- Mobile marketing consulting

Please check out our website at:
www.FirstMobileWebsite.com

Ready, Set, Go!

You've read about a lot of different mobile marketing strategies in this book – from SMS to proximity marketing to QR codes, and everything in between. Now it's your turn to put these strategies to work. In the next section we'll give you solid reasons to make this move, and provide you with some closing advice on how to get started.

It's Your Turn

This book has given you a plethora of mobile marketing ideas, all of which are backed up by "real life" case studies from companies that have already gotten their feet wet in this growing marketing space.

Now it's your turn. Whether you want to launch a simple, inexpensive SMS text campaign targeted at existing customers, or roll out a multi-faceted mobile marketing campaign that ties into your website, the world is literally your oyster. The opportunities are limitless, and range from those that take just a few minutes and a few dollars to implement, to more elaborate campaigns that cost a little more money and require you to enlist expert help to get the job done.

If you don't believe that now is the time to get into the mobile marketing game, consider these statistics from the Mobile Marketing Association. In its Mobile Advertising Trends 2011 report, the MMA reveals that:

✓ Asia is still the leader in mobile advertising and will proceed with being the strongest market in terms of ad spending. In 2010 Japanese companies already invested more than $1 billion in this business followed by South Korea and China ($270M and $180M). In Asia more than 15 billion page impressions are being generated on a daily basis in mobile.

✓ The U.S. is the second largest market globally in terms of mobile advertising spending behind Japan. It will close the gap next year with a forecast of $1.24 billion, and will grow to $5 billion in 2015.

✓ The top 5 European countries (UK, Italy, France, Germany, and Spain) will see a huge increase in mobile ad spending. At the end of 2010 these "Big Five" were estimated to have 65 million mobile Internet users; this number will more than double within the next 5 years up to 160 million. The "Big Five" will reach the $1 billion mark approximately in 2014.

Now that you have a few ideas of how mobile marketing might work for your company, it's time to come up with a successful game plan. Start by looking at how mobile marketing can be integrated into your current marketing mix (print ads, direct mail, TV and radio advertisements) and how it can replace and/or augment those existing channels.

Remember that mobile marketing is all about stoking user engagement. Unlike the magazine ad that "speaks" to the reader without asking him or her to actually get involved with the company placing the ad, mobile marketing is a two-way street. Because of this, it's important to keep your audience in mind when developing your campaigns, and then as you tap the medium's measurability to accountability tools to tweak your mobile marketing efforts to perfection.

Good luck!

50 Trusted Mobile Marketing Resources

Leading text and multimedia messaging application providers:

Cellyspace (cellyspace.com)

Club Texting (clubtexting.com)

Ez Texting (eztexting.com)

iLoop Mobile (iloopmobile.com)

Mobile Interactive Group (migcan.com)

Mobilizeus (mobilizeus.com)

Mogreet (mogreet.com)

Trumpia (trumpia.com)

Vibes Media (vibes.com)

Velti (velti.com)

Waterfall Mobile (waterfallmobile.com)

Leading mobile advertising providers:

Admob (admob.com)

Crisp Wireless (crispwireless.com)

iAD Network (advertising.apple.com)

JumpTap (jumptap.com)

Millennial Media (millenialmedia.com)

Smaato (smaato.com)

Leading social networks that are being accessed via mobile:

Buzzd (buzzd.com)

Brightkite (brightkite.com)

Facebook (facebook.com)

Foursquare (Foursquare.com)

Google Latitude (google.com/latitude)

Gowalla (gowalla.com)

Loopt (loopt.com)

MocoSpace (mocospace.com)

Twitter (twitter.com)

Yelp (yelp.com)

Leading QR generators:

Kerem Erkan (keremerkan.net/qr-code-and-2d-code-generator/)

Mobile-barcodes (mobile-barcodes.com/qr-code-generator/)

Qurify (qurify.com/en/)

Leading QR code browser extensions:

Firefox plug-in (addons.mozilla.org/en-US/firefox/addon/mobile-barcoder/)

Google Chrome (chrome.google.com/extensions/detail/bcfddoencoie dfjgepnlhcpfikgaogdg)

Leading QR code solution providers:

Bcode (bcode.com)

Jagtag (jagtag.com)

NeoMedia (neom.com)

Neustar (neustar.com)

Quickmark (quickmark.cn)

Scanlife (web.scanlife.com)

Leading Bluecasting and Proximity Marketing providers:

Ad-pods (ad-pods.com)

AURA (aura.net.au/)

BLIP Systems (blipsystems.com)

Blue Giga (bluegiga.com)

Blue Blitz (blueblitz.com)

Waymedia (mobitouchcube.com)

*Leading do-it-yourself and cross platform
application developers:*

Do it yourself:

AppBreeder (appbreeder.com)

My AppBuilder (myappbuilder.com)

Magmito (magmito.com)

App Developers:

Grapple (grapplemobile.com)

Mutual Mobile (mutualmobile.com)

Sencha Touch (sencha.com)